Stress Free Teaching

A practical guide to tackling stress in teaching, lecturing and tutoring

Stress Free Teaching

A practical guide to tackling stress in teaching, lecturing and tutoring

RUSSELL JOSEPH

KOGAN
PAGE

First published in 2000

Kogan Page Limited
120 Pentonville Road
London
N1 9JN
UK

Stylus Publishing Inc.
22883 Quicksilver Drive
Sterling
VA 20166–2012
USA

British Library Cataloguing in Publication Data

A CIP record for this book is available from the British Library.

ISBN 0 7494 3114 8

Typeset by Saxon Graphics Ltd, Derby
Printed and bound in Great Britain by Clays Ltd, St Ives plc

Contents

Preface

Research has shown that those in the professions, particularly helping professions, have significantly high levels of stress. This book identifies some of the issues faced by those in the education sector.

Those employed in education have been under increasing pressure and unrelenting criticism for many years. Critics have failed to recognize that there is an increasing complexity and responsibility with regard to education. Apparently overgenerous terms and conditions of employment have been replaced with new, less favourable contracts and more responsibilities. This has resulted in the removal of what the public regards as luxurious short working weeks and lengthy holidays, and a general lack of support and recognition for the contributions the sector makes to society. The ecology of the school, college or university has changed and is now significantly different from previous generations. It is not difficult to understand why teachers and lecturers are susceptible to stress.

One particular concern is the apparent attitude that stress is not recognized as a problem needing to be solved. Sadly many, including those managing others, fail to recognize that a problem exists. It is not a personal soapbox issue of the 'victims'. There is no quick fix remedy to this denial. Yet realization will bring about its own rewards through motivation, increased co-operation, lower absence and an enhanced attitude towards employment.

This book aims to help those who provide education and those who manage people providing education. It is not about teaching as a job or the skills necessary in order to teach, but is aimed at recognizing that stress in education exists and offers support to those who might need it. The intention is for it to be easily read, yet with ideas for you to try to see if they work for you. The last thing a potentially stressed teacher wants is to struggle through a heavily laden text trying to comprehend the measures necessary for reducing stress. Teachers have enough to do.

Chapters 1, 2 and 3 identify the cause and effect of stress in both general and educational environments. These chapters provide a foundation for the book and highlight the implications of negative stress on a personal and organizational level.

Chapter 4 looks at the legal implications of working in a stressful situation. This includes employers' responsibilities and obligations as well as the measures that an employee may be able to take to remedy the situation.

Stress reduction strategies begin in Chapter 5 by approaching stress as a management issue at varying levels of authority, remembering that many teachers are managers of programme areas as well as members of the teaching teams involved. Chapter 6 reveals personal coping strategies for the teacher, considering the changes in curriculum and the change in culture of education detailed in Chapter 3.

Chapter 7 identifies general stress reduction techniques that may prove useful in addition to the education-specific approaches mentioned in Chapter 6. Case studies from a broad spectrum of teachers across education, each giving their own remedies, can be found in the final chapter.

For the purpose of this text a 'teacher' is the name given to anyone providing education at any level, including those who lecture and those who are tutors.

Good luck. I hope you achieve your aims.

Acknowledgements

I would like to pay tribute to the many people who have helped with this book. Everyone has been under extreme pressure, the very nature of the topic, and my appreciation goes to those involved in the original workshop session and to all those who completed a research questionnaire.

My appreciation also extends to staff at schools, colleges and universities and to those people from industry who also gave their time, thoughts and emotions.

Finally, I thank everyone else who has been supportive. The high level of interest is a demonstration of the importance people attach to this work.

Introduction

In September 1999 a High School teacher was awarded £47,000 from her employer, the local authority, for the stress she suffered. The out-of-court settlement is believed to be the first proven case of stress involving teachers. The teacher, Muriel Benson, was supported in her action by the National Union of Teachers, which is currently supporting up to 100 other teachers in their actions against their employers. The union argued that as a result of this settlement, teacher stress was proven to be an occupational health hazard.

The basis for Mrs Benson's claim was that she worked in excess of 60 hours each week and it was this that had made her ill. Her employer argued that she was a victim of her own success as more pupils chose her subject – media studies.

Although the employer did not admit liability, an out-of-court settlement was reached after Mrs Benson alleged that her employer failed to carry out a duty of care to employees.

Mrs Benson was an enthusiastic teacher who taught a range of students, ran after-school activities, concerts and an annual poetry festival as well as having pastoral care duties as head of year. Each day would mean 9 or 10 hours on the school premises and a further two or three hours marking and preparation. One day each weekend was taken up with more schoolwork.

Despite writing to her employers about her workload, she was not supported and at times was given extra work. She felt that her employers took advantage of her enthusiasm, initiative and commitment. As a result of the stress she suffered, Mrs Benson took early retirement at the age of 57. Her career over, she still has difficulty focusing on aspects of her everyday life and grieves for the loss of a career that she loved.

So what makes teaching stressful?

I'm having a bad dream. I arrive at college at 8 am. Today shouldn't be too bad. I only have five hours contact time. Five hours with a group of students. This includes one hour tutorial with my own group. The rest of the time I plan to do some marking and lesson preparation. I don't officially start until 9 am. I am paid for a 36-hour week, but college management refuses to recognize that I start before 9 am and so my time before then is unpaid.

The first thing I do is check my e-mails. I have to do this early because I share my staffroom with five others. We have one computer to share and if I don't log on early I won't get a chance until midday. I have seven new messages since leaving at 6 pm the previous evening. My line manager has called a divisional meeting for 1 pm. It's my lunch hour. But it seems to be important, as have all the other meetings that have taken place during my lunch hour. The second e-mail concerns my first class. College management wants to amalgamate another group of students into this group. They are, I am told, a small group of six who cannot be taught alone because of financial constraints.

My first class is at 9 am. I should have 45 students, including the new 6. There are only 17. The rest are late or absent. The students are now in four vocational groups but come together for my subject – a business subject that is an integral part of each of their vocational programmes. Sometimes it gets difficult because I have to angle the subject matter to each of the specialisms. By 9.15, another 15 students arrive. No apology, no excuse apart from 'it's the buses'.

'Get an earlier bus.'

'No! You can't expect me to leave home any earlier. It's not my problem.'

Today is assignment day. I have to issue assignments to all four vocational groups, go through each and every task that they have to do and explain what is wanted in order for them to be successful. This takes forever because I now have four specialist groups each looking at the assignment from a different angle.

Once completed, we begin the day's classroom work. Damn, the overhead projector has just blown a fuse. Call media resources. 'Sorry, we can't help you until 11 am.' My class is only until 10.50.

'Today we are going to carry on from last week's lesson. Can you get out that work, please, and pass the homework forward to me.'

'I wasn't here last week.'

'But you caught up the work in your own time, didn't you?'

A blank look. 'It's not my fault I was sick.'

'I don't understand . . . '

'That's because you didn't catch up.'

War of words continues.

I use one of the new marker pens. Luckily I have two. That's a relief because one of them doesn't work. In the past we had to return one empty pen whenever we wanted a replacement. Board marker pen security was so tight. What did management think we wanted them for? Selling on the black market? A case of no trust.

My next class is at 11.10 and so I get time for a quick coffee break. As I go to leave my staffroom the telephone rings. It's the parents of one of my students. The parents are concerned that their child is working too hard, leaving home before 7 in the morning and not getting home again in the evenings until 9 pm. They argue that the work is too intense. Are we talking about the same student? The student by that name is rarely in college and is falling very far behind. I finally realize that the student has a new boyfriend, of another religion/nationality, and that they must be together most of the day. The parents are none the wiser. What should I do? What am I trained to do? Am I a trained counsellor?

The coffee break I had planned is over and so I head off to my next class. This group is what we describe as pre-level 2. Most are new to this country and have learning difficulties or special needs. It is very difficult going from one 'A' level-equivalent group to another group of students at this level of ability. The majority of the group have a common language, not English. At home they don't speak English. At college they try not to. Three are absent. Apparently they are acting as interpreters for their families who do not speak English.

As the class begins there is a knock on the door. One of the students from my tutor group is there, wanting to speak to me. She is clearly distressed. Should I turn her away? Should I leave an exercise for the students to get on with? After a few minutes the upset student calms down and will see me during the tutorial.

As I turn back to face my class I see Nigel showing his friends his new toy. Unlike most of his peers it's not a new mobile phone and they are not sharing a piece of chewing gum. And this isn't a woodwork class, so why is Nigel carving his name into the desk with a knife that looks lethal? Calmly I go up to Nigel.

'That looks impressive,' I say, 'can I see it?'

As I take it away, Nigel hasn't realized that there could be a problem. I call security. Nigel is suspended from college. He vows to 'get me'. If not me, I think maybe my car!

The class ends at midday and I finally get time for a quick coffee which I leave to cool down while I go and do some photocopying. I am held up in the copying room because one of the machines has broken down. By the time I return to my staffroom, the coffee is cold. On the way I pass by the main office to collect my post. Two ex-students, from five years before, want references. What were they like? Luckily I have records of their results and a copy of their application forms to remind me. Another letter is from a prospective student. He wants information and an application form for one of my courses. The return address is a young persons' detention centre. There is no mention as to the problem behind his detention but I decide that it is important that I at least know in case he puts any of my other students in a dangerous situation. At least he will have a social worker who I can deal with should the need arise!

The meeting at 1 pm is lively. College management want results and analysis from our respective courses – by the end of the day. They have already had the results three times.

'I agree, but this time they want them in a different format.'

We have little choice as college funding is dependent on results. Other agenda items include: external examinations; new students discipline procedures; new registers systems; education inspectors' proposed visits; new course development; a discussion on a proposed visit with students at a weekend; a careers convention over several evenings; a prize-giving evening; and specific students' problems and progress. The meeting ends at 1.55 pm. Just in time for my 2 pm tutorial.

Claire is pregnant. Her parents don't know. Her boyfriend is black, she is white. Her parents are racist. What should she do? What should I do?

Justin is finding it hard to keep up with college work. He lives at home with his mother. The father left them after years of abuse. They have little money and Justin has two jobs to help support his family. He is only just 18 and wants to work in tourism but each morning he is a cleaner in a nearby office block and each afternoon after college he stacks shelves at the local supermarket. He has little time for college work.

Elena is a model student. She is from Belarus and is here to study tourism. English isn't her first language but she tries hard. She has little family support as they are still in Belarus. Her work experience was in a travel agency/tour operator. They want to keep her on a full-time basis but she doesn't know what is best for her. She wants the money but should she give up college? We have a long discussion about the opportunities for her and I try to get her to talk to her employers about working part-time rather than full-time. This has happened many times before. Good students are often 'poached' by their work experience employer with the offer of a good wage, time off for training and part-time college courses. The bonus and opportunities rarely materialize and students end up worse off than if they had stayed at college and completed their course.

I am supposed to keep written records of all tutorials for future reference. Some things are just too personal to be kept in a file on my desk. 'And don't forget the Data Protection Act,' argued the human resource manager at a previous meeting. Do I keep these sensitive records then? Or not? Do I have a lockable drawer?

Finally I get to go to the loo. While in there I see a project coming towards me under the door. A student didn't want it to be late and wanted to catch me before he went home. I leave the toilet and bump into a girl who should have been in my class the previous day.

'Where were you yesterday?' I say.

'My iron broke,' she replied.

'So?' I was somewhat perplexed.

'I had to go and buy a new one.'

'What's that got to do with college?'

'You don't expect me to come in to college with clothes not ironed, do you?'

This student had been absent a number of times with silly excuses. She was about to go on work experience and so I thought that before she went out to represent herself and us I should contact her father to see if there was an underlying problem affecting her work and attitude.

Her father was an employer, employing over 50 people in his factory.

'I understand that your daughter wasn't in college because she had to go out and buy a new iron?'

'If that's what she told you, that's the truth.'

The conversation went on and on. We agreed to differ. He thought it important that his daughter should do whatever she thought was right, even buying a new iron. As an employer, as long as his employees told him the truth, even if they went off to buy their own iron, in his time, he would pay them. I couldn't win. So much for parental support!

As I head off down the corridor towards my last class I am stopped three times by colleagues. Each one wants some of my time. Do I have a handout on. . .? Can we discuss. . . ? When are you free to look at new courses? The list is endless.

My last class of the day is to a group of Higher National Diploma students. They are quite bright and it is an immense change from the class earlier. Change? Is that the right word? Challenge may be better. It can be very difficult adapting from those who have learning difficulties to those approaching degree level.

During the day I have taught six groups of students at different levels in addition to the tutorial group. So much for planning and preparation as well as marking. At least I can do some now, before tonight's careers evening event. And if it's not all finished, I can always do some when I get home at 9 pm. Meanwhile, what should I say to Claire, Justin and Elena?

1 Is there stress in education?

Chapter goals

This chapter focuses on change and questions the existence of stress in education. It introduces the possibility of contributory factors including:

- changes in society;
- technological developments;
- changing student needs;
- the new business culture of education;
- teaching being a paradigm.

The arrival of the twenty-first century and the millennium celebration have given us the perfect opportunity to reflect on the past. We see that the world we live in is changing. The fundamental rules that we live by have been altered dramatically. What was right in the seventies and eighties may be inappropriate now. Conversely, what we now view as acceptable may have been out-of-line with the world in the 1960s. Some examples of these changes include:

- the development and necessity of the mobile phone;
- the emergence of information as a key resource;
- the loss of respect for politicians, royalty and the police;

▌ cohabitation instead of marriage;
▌ gay parenting;
▌ digital television;
▌ smaller and faster personal computers;
▌ new pricing strategies amongst airlines;
▌ safe sex;
▌ the Internet.

But what do all these changes mean? Anticipating change would have given countless opportunities. At the very least there would be less 'future' shock as the changes come about. Society works within boundaries – what is acceptable and what is not. Changes are less likely to cause shock if they are foreseen or expected. They are less painful if they are deemed necessary; if they are seen as appropriate.

The boundaries surrounding education are no different. These boundaries include:

▌ the student;
▌ the parents;
▌ employers;
▌ education managers;
▌ the government;
▌ administrators;
▌ assessments;
▌ grading;
▌ league tables;
▌ inspections.

All the above boundaries want the best for students – the achievers of tomorrow. Yet in many cases they fail to provide them with the resources, and support, to carry out their tasks.

Education is a vocation. It is a job with a difference. In most organizations, whether service or product orientated, the process begins with a raw material. This raw material then goes through a transition using a variety of resources, tools or equipment until it reaches an end product; in education, a successful student. The main tools, resources and equipment involved in adding value to the student are called teachers, tutors and lecturers. Throughout the process of adding value to the students, the 'resources' are bombarded with the human element including student behaviour, staff contracts, new courses, new assessment procedures and paperwork.

Most jobs have elements of difficulty, yet research has shown that jobs in the service sector, ie jobs involving meeting members of the public, are prone to more stress than most.

Education is now a business. More so than at any time in the past. As a result, one of the most significant changes is the need to keep students no matter what the level of behaviour and ability. Visions of financial opportunity abound, the cash register rings with the hope of a full-time student progressing through the census points for funding methodology. This role change, the development of corporate responsibility, self-management and 'supervised' rule, has brought about huge advances and a 'mission' leading to change and the next millennium.

So where now? Culture, environment, strategy, human resource policy and management style all change and by their nature affect staff. But change and the management of change is a significant catalyst for an ever-increasing problem caused by these changes.

If a teacher could visualize the journey, it would be on several tracks leading to the same destination. The emerging bureaucracy called education has ensured that there is little time for teaching and preparation and many more administrative tasks. To be successful many teachers find themselves constantly 'chasing their tail' – juggling tasks, following up. Changing courses and developments demand that programmes are continually reviewed, monitoring the environment to ensure commercial activities are not missed. Further and higher education try to work alongside industry to develop short, full-cost courses to improve financial prospects.

In many areas, especially inner cities, a further problem is that students have less enthusiasm and willingness than before. They have higher expectations, but these are based on what they should be given in return for very little effort. Where does this stem from? Can we lay the blame on the whole education system? Or is life in general moving so fast that we don't have time for ourselves and our children?

So teachers who have to 'chase their tail', cope with students and their changing needs, deal with a fast moving and changing environment, adopt new standards and qualifications, may find themselves in stressful situations. Teaching is a stressful profession and the radical changes currently occurring within the education system are likely to increase rather than decrease the levels of stress.

Is stress a fad? Is the individual to blame?

There is a danger that stress is seen as a fad – a pathological state, where there must be something wrong with the individual. Most middle managers' jobs are quite stressful; many work in excess of 60 hours a week. Many don't get long holidays to recuperate. So what makes teaching different? Could it be that, when the middle managers were in schools and colleges, the culture of education was significantly different? The difference is this: all teachers experience stress to some degree and this is the result of their interaction and interdependence with the environment in which they work.

To answer whether this is simply a personal problem, there are two questions that need to be answered: what makes teaching as a profession stressful and what makes some teachers become stressed?

The answer is clear – one is situational and one personal. If everything goes well, parents and employers think their students are good pupils, but if things go badly, they think the teacher is bad! Not only bad teachers experience stress and not only good teachers avoid stress – it will undoubtedly depend on the conditions and environment in which teachers work, or in their own ability to cope with varying situations.

Education is undergoing great changes in all areas of its contextual environment. Each of the component parts in the example below could establish an area for investigation. While managers have time, opportunity and experience to deal with these changes, many of the implications are being experienced by those *delivering* the programmes and systems of work. The success of the acceptance of these changes, and the embedding of these new developments, play a part in the future growth of schools, colleges and universities. Co-ordinating a few changes requires time and patience, but changes on the scale which the education sector is experiencing may bring increased levels of confusion, anxiety and occupational stress. There is a clear requirement to develop a strategy to implement change effectively and efficiently while considering the needs of those who deliver its primary purpose, education.

Is teaching a paradigm?

Before answering this question, it is firstly necessary to understand what a paradigm is. There are several definitions but broadly speaking a paradigm is a set of rules – a framework by which people operate; a framework of thought. Some people refer to a paradigm as a method of perception – the way in which we see things. If you look up the word in a dictionary you discover that it comes from the Greek *paradeigma*, which means 'model, pattern, example'.

Proof that teaching is a paradigm is this: teaching is now stressful. It hasn't always been and it might not always be. There are reasons for this in Chapter 3 and these are the boundaries in which teaching operates. This is the paradigm. Slowly, negative stress is being recognized as a problem. Education exists within a thought process of what is right and what is wrong, what is acceptable and what is not. The rules of teaching have changed and the boundaries are in a different position. Teaching lives in a world of paradigm shifts. Paradigms are the key not just to change, but also to innovation and development. This has been what teaching is all about. The rules have changed and will change again. Meanwhile teachers need to be open to looking to the changes, exploring them for their implications and creating a support climate. Suggestions to help do this can be found in Chapters 7 and 8.

Educational reports   Industry

New course
development

The environment of the further   Examining
education college   bodies

Qualifications   College
                                             funding

Role of the educator

Figure 1.1 The environment of the further education college

How can we increase effectiveness?

To promote effectiveness in education, it is necessary to:

▌ understand the implications of positive and negative stress;
▌ enable employers and individuals to recognize stress;
▌ recognize the symptoms of stress in education;
▌ classify an individual's reaction to stress;
▌ identify situations in education highlighting stress;
▌ identify the common causes of stress in education;
▌ identify current coping strategies for stress in education.

The hypothesis

The ability of the education sector to generate positive stress, while experiencing major changes, will lead to more successful methods of teaching, raise student results and improve employee relations.

Do we need stress?

Stress is the dynamic force that makes us live. It causes us to stand, sit, speak, cry, work harder, work less and many other daily routines. It is not necessarily a negative emotion but has become a scapegoat to cover a number of situations. Stress is a relatively new concept in our culture and yet has quickly become recognized because professionals have been able to measure many physiological, biomechanical and clinical responses to it. They also understand why some people are more responsive and vulnerable to it. Those not able to cope with stress and stressful situations may suffer from diseases which, although not wholly attributed to stress, are often exaggerated by it.

Stress is part of normal life. Everyone suffers from it at some time and yet it is our ability to channel it which determines whether we are affected and to what extent. The degree of stress may be determined by external events and a person's perception of them. To one person, a situation may seem stimulating, but to another a heavy burden, and for this reason employers need to realize the difference between the effects of positive and negative stress.

2 *Identifying stress*

Chapter goals

This chapter deals with identifying stress in an individual and pays particular attention to:

▎ the four broad effects of negative stress;
▎ the comparison of pressure to stress;
▎ the body's reaction to stress.

What does the word 'stress' mean?

The word 'stress' is used loosely, with different people and different groups of people giving it a different emphasis – taking it to mean different things. Doctors, engineers, psychologists, management consultants and the general public all use the word in different ways. Engineers use it for load bearing, linguists for emphasis on syllables and doctors for something that we suffer from. It is unclear where the word stress comes from. One suggestion is that it comes from old French, *distresse*, meaning to be placed under narrowness or oppression. Over the centuries, this word changed to stress and distress; the first meaning somewhat ambivalent and the latter something unpleasant.

The meaning of the word really depends on what context it is used in. At one end of the scale, stress represents those challenges which excite and keep people on their toes. At the other end of the scale, stress represents those conditions under which individuals have demands placed upon them that they cannot physically or psychologically meet and which ultimately may lead to a breakdown. A definition could therefore be:

> Stress is an excess of demand made upon the adaptive capacities of the mind and body.

If these capacities can handle demand and enjoy the stimulation involved then stress is welcome and helpful. If they can't then stress is debilitating. Conclusively, stress can be both positive and negative. There is a wide variety of factors which may cause stress, known as stressors.

Who gets stressed?

Research suggests that servicemen, social workers, teachers and linguists have emerged as the biggest sufferers of rising stress in the 1990s. A study of over 100 occupations shows that these are among the jobs where workers have experienced the sharpest increases in worries about their workloads, deadline pressures, job security and responsibility. Therefore stress could be caused by lack of job security, downsizing, longer working hours and heavier workloads. As a consequence of additional hours, people are prone to health problems. The effect of downsizing is that a reduced workforce is burdened with the same number of tasks.

There is no simple way of predicting what will cause harmful levels of stress. People respond differently from one task to another; a repetitive job may be perceived by some as monotonous and boring while others enjoy the routine. Much depends on people's attitudes, experience, motivation and support groups. These may be at work, with family or friends. The identification of negative stress in an individual can be categorized in the four groups as shown in Table 2.1.

Table 2.1 Categories of some symptoms of negative stress

Physical	Emotional	Mental	Social
Rashes	Crying	Lack of interest	Lack of grooming
Headaches	Anxiety	Forgetfulness	Isolation
Teeth grinding	Frustration	Poor concentration	Loneliness
Fatigue	Nervousness	Low productivity	Lashing out
Colds	Depression	Negative attitude	Clamming up
Back and neck aches	Worry	Confusion	Lower sex drive
Stomach problems	Tension	No new ideas	Nagging
Insomnia	Mood swings	Lethargy	Fewer contacts
Increased use of drugs	Irritability	Easily discouraged	Using people

These lists are not exhaustive and clearly the physical symptoms are the most easily identified.

What is the difference between stress and pressure?

It has already been suggested that certain types of stress are motivational, stimulating and invigorating. This type of stress is generally known as pressure. A definition of pressure is that it is the type of reaction to a situation one has on realizing that one is able to handle it successfully – and which results in action and enthusiasm for newer challenges, achievement and the contentment of having good health. However, people's ability to deal with pressure is not limitless and too much pressure can have a detrimental effect and undermine the health of the workforce. When the going gets tough it is tempting to hide rather than face the situation. This is no solution and invariably exacerbates the situation as it intensifies the feelings of helplessness.

Destiny or personality?

Some employees may carry their own stress with them. Are neurotics more sensitive to all stresses than stable individuals? Although work and home conditions do affect stress, it may also be true that stress is influenced by personal factors such as personality traits, coping strategies and intelligence. It is suggested that people with negative effect, those with anxiety, irritability, neuroticism and self-depreciation, tend to be less productive, less job satisfied and more prone to absenteeism. These people appear to focus and dwell on the negative aspects of the world in general and experience more stress and are less able to cope with it.

The personality variable relates to the beliefs about internal or external control of reinforcement, that is, the control of behavioural outcomes. People who believe that the events which occur in their lives are a result of their own behaviour are said to have the expectancy of internal control, compared to those who believe that their lives are dependent on events outside their control, who are said to have an expectancy of external control. Managers and employees who have an internal _locus_ of control tend to see threatening events at work as being less stressful than those who have an external _locus_ of control and are subsequently more able to deal with the situation.

Consequences of stress

The consequences of stress are felt by the individuals, their families and the organizations they are involved in (either work or social). When demand outstrips capacity there may be both physiological and psychological reactions. Medical opinion estimates that between a half and three-quarters of all accidents and illnesses are negative stress related.

About 270,000 people take days off work because of stress each year. Insurers in the UK have seen a 90 per cent increase in mental and psychological claims over the past five years and are reluctant to pay out for the treatment of stress because of the difficulty of identifying it as a stand-alone physical condition.

In addition to the symptoms shown earlier, physical symptoms of stress may include:

■ hair loss;
■ eating disorders/bingeing;
■ tense, aching muscles and muscle pain;

❚ palpitations and chest discomfort;
❚ fainting;
❚ choking;
❚ indigestion and nausea;
❚ diarrhoea and frequent urination;
❚ tremors and twitching;
❚ breathlessness and overbreathing;
❚ tension headaches.

Sometimes stressful circumstances can give rise to symptoms of physical distress, pain or malfunctioning. If the stress response is not recognized for what it is and regarded as a possible sign of physical illness, this can cause a great deal of needless worry. Stress can produce a tremendous variety of physical symptoms and any part of the body can be upset. Chest discomfort or pain, diarrhoea, palpitations, headaches, and muscle twitches may all be signs of an increase in stress, as well as a dry mouth, sweaty palms, cold fingers and a knot in the stomach. Multiple complaints in a formerly uncomplaining person may be the first sign of increasing stress.

How does the body try to cope?

Many of the body's reactions to stress demands are useful as they prepare the body for the challenges facing it. The body reacts automatically in the following ways:

Energy mobilizers

❚ release into the bloodstream of adrenaline, a nonadrenaline from the adrenal glands. This acts as a stimulant, speeding up reflexes and providing increased capacity as responses are sharpened.
❚ release into the bloodstream of thyroid hormones from the thyroid gland, again to increase energy levels.
❚ release of cholesterol into the liver, aiding muscles function.

The downside is that permanent increases harden arteries and may lead to heart disease, liver malfunction and exhaustion in the long term.

Energy support systems

- shut down of digestive system, allowing for blood to be diverted to the heart and lungs.
- blood is diverted from the skin for use elsewhere and sweat is produced to cool muscles overheated by rush of energy.
- air passages in the lungs dilate, allowing the blood to take up more oxygen.

The downside is that prolonged stomach shut down leads to stomach disorders, oversweating causes a breakdown in the body's thermostat and too much oxygen may cause fainting.

Concentration aids

- release into the blood stream of endorphins to act as natural painkillers.
- senses become more acute.
- sex hormone production reduces.

The downside is that when there is a prolonged effect, the effects may cause depression, breathing problems and impotence.

Too much stress

Certain levels of stress are beneficial until they go past capacity levels. The cognitive effects of too much stress can be identified as:

- lack of concentration and poor attention span;
- easily distracted;
- reduced memory;
- response speeds become unpredictable;

■ errors increase;
■ organization and planning skills deteriorate.

The emotional effects can be:

■ physical and psychological tensions increase;
■ hypochondria increase;
■ change in personality;
■ depression and helplessness appear;
■ reduction in self-esteem.

General behavioural effects are:

■ speech problems increase;
■ less enthusiasm;
■ absenteeism increases;
■ low energy levels;
■ disrupted sleep;
■ shifting of responsibilities;
■ problems are solved artificially;
■ suicide attempts.

Conclusion

The following conclusions may be drawn:

■ Negative stress causes and is caused by poor relationships.
■ Negative stress lowers productivity and may make people inefficient.
■ Major bodily systems such as the autonomic nervous system, endocrine and immune systems may be affected.
■ There will be an increase in sickness absence.
■ Some people will be unable to make (quality) decisions and their decision response time will become unreliable.
■ Lower morale.
■ Reduced quality of output.

Stressor + stress + strain may equal burnout, a state of mental and physical exhaustion as a result of long-term stress. It is important to recognize the signs and symptoms of stress both personally and occupationally; the diversity and control of stress may be due to a person's internal/external control.

Individuals may show quite different signs and symptoms when exposed to the same stressors and if an individual reacts poorly to stress they may exacerbate the situation. It must be remembered that psychological stresses can trigger physical symptoms.

3 *Occupational stress*

Chapter goals

This chapter is in three parts. Part 1 looks at the issues people face at work, including:

▌ the challenges imposed by management;
▌ stressful features in a job;
▌ examples of stressful jobs.

Part 2 pays attention to the stressors faced by teachers, in particular:

▌ student behaviour;
▌ parental support;
▌ issues relating to employment conditions;
▌ role conflict and ambiguity.

Each sector of the education system is reviewed in Part 3, broadly defined as:

▌ primary, junior and secondary schools;
▌ further education;
▌ higher education.

PART 1
Issues people face at work

Challenges imposed by management

A traditional view is often that stress is a dirty word, one that employers and managers don't want to acknowledge. Many feel that if the stress is brought to work from another source, such as the home or family environment, it is not the responsibility of the employer to deal with it. It is far easier to avoid other people's emotional problems with the excuse that they are personal and not related to the business. The natural reaction is often to ignore it and hope that it will go away.

Broadly speaking, our jobs become ever more complicated as the nature of work and society in general becomes more complicated and sophisticated. Many people look at the salaries and benefits of middle and senior managers with envy. But the rewards are high because the costs are high too. There are inevitably downsides, difficulties and drawbacks – often resulting in chronic stress (over a long period) or acute stress (extreme amounts).

In many management jobs, leaders are both supported and challenged. Supported by peers, subordinates and superiors who then challenge them to work harder. This can be broadly categorized in the following way:

▌ _Much support and little challenge_. Managers in this role have good technical and social support but as a result of being underchallenged are often stressed by boredom and monotony.
▌ _Much support, much challenge_. This combination tends to get the most out of managers as they are challenged by superiors, customers, shareholders and other stakeholders to improve and are given substantial support to succeed.
▌ _Little support, much challenge_. This is an unfortunate and very common situation and a major cause of stress at work. The

employee is challenged to work harder but offered minimal support – emotionally, resourcefully or informationally.

▋ *Little support, little challenge.* In some bureaucracies, employees are given a quiet life, neither challenged nor supported. Consequently they remain stress free.

Stressful features in a job

Some jobs are more stressful than others. Certain features associated with particular jobs are stressful. For example, the greater the extent to which the job requires decision-making, constant monitoring of materials or machinery, in poor conditions, with repeated exchange information or unstructured jobs, the greater the degree of stress.

There are also other stressful features in a job, such as the following.

▋ *Role conflict.* Stress resulting from conflicting demands. From boss to friend, teacher to pastoral role, law enforcer to father confessor. This is a common practice among working mothers, human resource personnel and teachers. The adverse effects of role conflict may be less pronounced in work settings that are characterized by friendliness and social support compared to occupations where these work support settings are excluded.

▋ *Role ambiguity.* Stress resulting from uncertainty, often as a result of employees being unaware of what is expected of them through a lack of a job description or specified responsibilities. They may be unaware of several aspects of their job or how to divide their time between various tasks. Ambiguity also results from changes in the organization and the profession.

▋ *Over- and underload stress.* Stress resulting from having too little or too much to do. Work overload can be quantitative or qualitative. The former is where the work required is too much within the given time. The latter is when employees feel that they do not possess sufficient resources, skills or ability to do the job. Quantitative underload leads to boredom when employees have too little to do, whereas qualitative underload is a result of the tasks being repetitive and without mental stimulation.

- *Responsibility for others.* Many employees are responsible for others, needing to motivate and reward, punish and correct and, most importantly, communicate. This often causes considerable stress when facing human aspects such as dealing with organizational policies, complaints and exercising leadership.
- *Lack of social support.* This is the stress caused by being isolated and ignored. Having friends and supporters in times of difficulty helps employees and managers see threatening events as more controllable. They may also suggest strategies for dealing with situations and coping techniques. This type of support can be qualitative and quantitative; the former being the more beneficial although copious amounts of both are ideal.
- *Lack of participation in decisions.* Many people in junior and middle management feel isolated because they are not involved in a decision-making process that may directly affect their job.
- *Poor performance appraisal.* Stress from little or no feedback, or from a biased report. The problem in a minimal appraisal system is that staff do not know how they are doing, or should be doing. A negative appraisal without being told how to improve also increases stress levels.
- *Working conditions.* Some jobs have to be done in poor and often difficult conditions. These include jobs in extreme temperatures, such as mining, or with loud noise, such as road digging.
- *Organizational change.* This is the stress that comes from adapting to new techniques and methods of work. As the speed, type and amount of organizational change occur, so the level of stress increases. Changes in policy, reorganizing and mergers all lead to uncertainty and, consequently, stress.
- *Career development.* Many people at work live in the hope of advancement based on seniority and performance. Staff build up their hopes and expectations and, if these are thwarted, this raises levels of stress.
- *Home/work interface.* Traditionally associated with women, this conflict of home and work demands may result in divided loyalties. This is most serious when neither environment is tolerant or supportive.

Examples of stressful jobs

Within any business there is no thing as a pressure-free job. Pressure in the workplace is an unavoidable fact of life bringing with it its own responsibilities and problems.

Research has shown that a number of jobs are frequently associated with negative stress.

Table 3.1 High stress jobs

High stress jobs because of danger, extreme pressure, or having responsibility without control	High stress jobs because of 'occupational' risk of depression serious enough to require therapy
Air traffic controller	Air traffic controller
Customer service or complaints	Artistic performer
Department worker	Clergyman
Inner-city high school teacher	Computer programmer
Journalist	Dentist
Medical intern	Government worker
Miner	Lawyer
Police officer	Middle manager
Secretary	Physician
Stockbroker	Police officer
Waitress	Politician
Therapist	*Teacher*

Conclusion

Causes of stress at work

The general causes of stress at work are:

- organizational problems;
- insufficient backup and support;
- long or unsociable hours;
- poor pay, status and promotion prospects;
- apparently unnecessary procedures;
- unclear job specification;
- role conflict;
- unrealistic expectations;

∎ inability to influence decision-making processes;
∎ isolation;
∎ poor leadership;
∎ difficult clients;
∎ insufficient training.

Effects of stress at work

The effects of stress at work are:

∎ poor industrial relations;
∎ reduced output;
∎ lack of concentration;
∎ poor decision-making;
∎ inability to associate with colleagues, managers, and subordinates;
∎ frustration;
∎ increased absenteeism;
∎ lower productivity;
∎ reduced quality of output;
∎ lower morale;
∎ less enthusiasm, team spirit and conscientiousness.

PART 2
Stress in education

Student behaviour

> All human behaviour has a cause which in itself is a com-
> bined effect of heredity and environment.
> *Psychologists' assumptions*

Does this include codes of conduct and discipline? Establishing acceptable standards of behaviour?

Somewhere in a British school, college or university at least one teacher or lecturer will be assaulted tomorrow. The number of incidents in which pupils, their parents or other relatives set about their teachers is growing alarmingly. The Suzy Lamplugh Trust published a report which found that 1 in 10 pupils carry dangerous weapons. High profile cases such as the killing of headteacher Philip Lawrence and the Dunblane tragedy are well known. Other incidents, happening on almost a daily basis, are mainly unpublicized.

Student behaviour is one of the major factors which contribute to the stress, demoralization and dropout of teachers and lecturers in education. The need to cope with the pressures of the profession is not necessarily a new problem, but it has been significantly magnified by the nature of our society and education in the current social system. The expectations of, and the demands on, educators today are immensely different from the past. A study in Milwaukee, USA, revealed a striking contrast between the problems faced in the 1940s and the 1980s. The 1940s problems have not faded away, they are simply no longer thought to be serious.

Studies of what teachers described as disruptive behaviour were also conducted in two London secondary schools. When these teachers talked about acts of disruption, they meant rowdiness, abuse, bad language, talking and refusing to accept the teacher's authority. In these schools, disruptive behaviour did not take the form of violence and aggression towards teachers.

Table 3.2 Problems facing teachers

In the 1940s	In the 1980s
Talking out of turn	Drug abuse
Chewing gum	Alcohol abuse
Making noises	Pregnancy
Running in the corridors	Suicide
Jumping the queue	Rape
Violating the dress code	Robbery
Dropping litter	Assault

Specific examples of student behaviour which makes difficult demands on staff have been given recently:

- arriving late;
- distracting other pupils;
- asking to go to the toilet repeatedly;
- missing lessons, absconding;
- smoking in toilets;
- rude remarks under breath;
- refusing to do set work;
- playing with matches;
- cheeky remarks to teachers;
- talking when supposed to be writing;
- fighting in class;
- open abuse to teachers;
- packing up early as if to leave;
- defacing books;
- failing to complete homework;
- graffiti;
- bizarre clothing and make-up;
- threatening teachers;
- hitting teachers;
- rocking on chairs defiantly.

One of the most extensive and influential investigations into the causes and effects of disruptive behaviour in the 1980s was the Elton Report (Department of Education and Science and Welsh

Office, 1989). The results of this research indicated that the most disturbing pupil behaviour experienced by teachers includes talking out of turn, hindering other pupils, making unnecessary noises, work avoidance, not being punctual and getting up out of a seat without permission. When these examples of disruptive behaviour are compared with more serious problems such as verbal abuse and aggression or vandalism, they appear insignificant as a cause of stress. This could be true if they were isolated incidents, but for teachers they cause frequent frustrations and hassles during the working day.

The student is a customer

A further stress issue is that, in the growing business culture of further and higher education, students are seen as *customers*. Many educational institutions now have a performance monitoring system which often takes the form of a module or course assessment by the students. The purpose of this is to identify good and bad teachers and develop a customer-focused strategy. This assessment process, evaluating the ability of the teacher, could be open to abuse. Accepting that students want high grades in order to secure passes and future opportunities, it is recognized that teachers also want the students to do well and report back favourably. Some less able students may see an assessment of the teacher as an opportunity to increase their own grades. Blackmail, even in a covert form, may exist, with the teacher being unwilling to fail poor students for fear of being punished with a damning assessment that may have a bearing on their own promotion, pay or self-esteem.

Key issues

Lecturers in further and higher education often teach on a number of different programmes, dealing with many courses – each adopting different codes of conduct. Students typically play one lecturer off against another by expressing the view that some behaviour is acceptable by one and so should be acceptable by all. This may become argumentative, which leads to less teaching and a resulting cumulative effect. Students are confused and need parameters of discipline which all lecturers can work to, are understood, and are accepted by staff, students and their parents.

The following table identifies areas for discussion and development:

Table 3.3   Student behaviour

Student behaviour	Symptoms/ effect on output	Symptoms/effect on lecturer	Possible treatment
Poor attendance	Falling behind	Disruption to programme	Enforcement of attendance rules Letters to parents Use of industry-led disciplinary procedures
Lateness	Disruption to classmates	Disruption to lecturer	1. Exclusion and marked absent 2. Lateness penalties
Submission of late work	Falling behind	Disruption to marking procedures	Uniform penalty enforced
Chewing gum	Unacceptable to industry	Unable to facilitate to industry standards	Uniform agreement/ policy
Hats	Unacceptable to industry – manners	Unable to facilitate to industry standards	Uniform agreement policy
Returning late from a break	Disruptive	Disruption to lecturer	Uniform policy/ agreement on breaks. Removal of privilege
Toilet breaks	Disruptive	Disruptive	Exceptionally
Terms of address – first name	Unacceptable to industry	Unacceptable to industry	Uniform policy/ agreement
Bad manners / answering back / disrespectful	Unacceptable to industry	Unacceptable to industry	Disciplinary procedures
Wearing of coats	Unwilling to commit	Disruptive	Uniform policy/ agreement

Conclusions

▪ students need parameters of behaviour and discipline;
▪ one-off events do not necessarily result in increased levels of stress;
▪ cumulative behavioural problems raise levels of stress;
▪ codes of conduct are not always implemented by staff;
▪ teachers and lecturers are under pressure, within a hostile environment, to improve results;
▪ increased class sizes cause stress and behavioural problems;
▪ lack of parental support increases stressors;
▪ industry needs to heighten awareness for the need of improved behaviour;
▪ lecturers in the further and higher education sector may not be trained to deal with poor behaviour;
▪ patterns of good behaviour may need to be instilled at an early age through home and family life.

Parental support

Many teachers like to meet the parents of their students. They want to form a rapport so that should a problem arise the cause of the problem can be solved and the student can return to studying. Sadly, this does not always happen. Teachers often complain about the lack of support and interest from the parents. This is often highlighted when there are special events at schools and colleges.

What is the reason for this? Many parents say that they are too busy, that they work during school/college hours, and so cannot attend school events. Is this because they are too busy in their own personal life or is it that they have no interest their child's education?

Some parents suggest that teachers are unqualified for the job. These people tend to be highly critical and become aggressive and sometimes abusive towards the teacher. They suggest that the child is not being taught well enough or that the teacher deals with situations wrongly. Such criticism makes the teacher despondent and upset, so leading to heightened levels of negative stress about their own self-worth and ability.

Some parents lie to teachers on behalf of their children. For example, some schools and colleges have a policy of contacting students if they are absent for a continued period. It is quite common for a parent to explain how the child has been very ill, confined to their bed, unable to eat or drink. (*Funny how they could get to the local disco last night, thinks the teacher!*) Similarly, some students lie for their parents. For example, some parents can never attend parents' evenings because they work in the evening. It could be that the parents are not interested or don't receive notice about the parents' evening. Some students lie about their parents.

'My parents never go to parents' evenings and so it's not worth asking them.'

'My grandmother is in hospital so my parents cannot come to school/college.'

'I live on my own, because my parents kicked me out.'

At what age should a parent stop being involved with their child's education? In truth, a good parent will never stop being involved and hopefully will play an active part in their development. Sadly, this isn't always the case. In general terms though, it is suggested that while students still live with their parents, education may benefit from co-operation between teacher and parent.

A poor or non-existent relationship between a parent and a teacher adds to the number of stressors the teacher encounters. Not only dealing with trying to teach, the teacher will lack the support and background knowledge of a potential problem or difficult situation. As a consequence, every time a student problem arises, the teacher, without clear instruction, will be pressured to deal with a situation with limited information, knowing that a poor decision may damage the situation further.

Employment conditions

Performance related pay

There are many industries and many jobs where employees get a bonus based on their performance. Factory workers may get piecework, paid by the number of 'pieces' that they manufacture. Salesmen may get a bonus based on the numbers of sales that they close. Airline cabin crew get a percentage of the sales they make when offering the duty-free trolley. But is performance related pay of use in the classroom?

Many staffroom discussions are about PRP and how a system could be implemented. Would it be on results? A bonus scheme, such as performance related pay is, suggests that it would be.

The questions then arise. . . If it is based on results, then teachers in areas that are geographically 'brighter' would have an advantage. This would lead to an exodus from inner-city schools. Would it be based on value added? In other words, would a bonus be paid on the added knowledge a student has at the end of the year? If so, would it be measured by exam results at the start and end of a course? Would a teacher of students with learning difficulties be disadvantaged and so venture back into mainstream schools and colleges for the bonus? Would teachers of certain age groups benefit more because students have greater capacity for learning once they can read and write? Would no one want to teach students new to the country? Would it be based on results? Would an unscrupulous teacher award more passes than before in order to secure their own bonus?

Teachers generally feel that PRP would be divisive and unrealistic. In many schools there is cynicism about the government's intention. But there is also concern. And this concern leads to stress.

The Department for Education and Employment (DfEE) argues that teachers will welcome PRP when it is fully detailed (*Times Educational Supplement*, January 2000). The view is that it will provide an opportunity for teachers to remain in the classroom and benefit from higher levels of pay without having to seek a management post to secure a higher salary. Currently, the only salary enhancement route is to leave the classroom situation and, given that many teachers enter the profession to impart knowledge in the classroom, education management may not be a preferred option. Meanwhile, the uncertainty about PRP adds to the burden faced by the classroom managers. The exact system has not been finalized but it is envisaged that some teachers will cross over the pay threshold and onto a greatly improved pay spine.

Advanced Skills teachers will have their own pay scales. The decision as to whether a teacher will be 'advanced' will be based on a performance review.

Pay

Teachers in England and Wales are paid according to the Teachers' Pay and Conditions Act 1991. Independent schools are not tied to these scales. Salaries are calculated on qualifications, experience and responsibilities. Some teachers are paid a bonus for excellence in teaching and learning. This bonus is decided by the governors of the employing school and often has an effect, both good and bad, on staff morale. Subjects and posts that are hard to fill may also be paid a bonus.

Lecturers in colleges and universities are paid according to their roles and responsibilities. The scale of pay often begins at circa £14,000 for a new member of the lecturing staff and may increase to £30,000 plus.

How is pay related to negative stress in teaching?

It is recognized and demanded that the teachers' role is to provide an education and training for employment. It is their excellence that is being conveyed to the pupils and students. It is their professional knowledge that is being passed on. In many cases, their contacts enable a graduating student to gain employment.

Some junior members of the teaching and lecturing profession are paid a similar amount or even less than their graduating students who have limited experience. Understandably, they find this distressing as they chose to come into teaching to pass on their expertise, only to find that industry would pay them more.

Administrative burden

A key source of stress within education is that of excessive paperwork. The time spent completing paperwork systems detracts from the quality time that could be spent with students, passing on knowledge. The limited time that teachers have is often felt to be wasted. Stress comes not only from completing the administrative load but also in the knowledge that other jobs still need to be done – including preparation and marking, both of which are the essential elements in providing education.

Most teachers have to deal with a series of bureaucratic systems at four levels for:

1. assessment;
2. funding requirements;
3. tracking;
4. inspection.

This is compounded by the fact that some of the data overlap and need to be presented in a variety of formats.

Description

Paperwork in the assessment level begins with the setting of a test or assignment. Systems vary according to the type of qualification and each qualification has a unique system (see Education Reports – Dearing). Teachers and lecturers involved on a number of teaching programmes may need to become familiar with each system. Each piece of work needs to cover a particular aspect of the syllabus, dealt with in terms of performance criteria and objectives. Within course teams, these pieces of work are monitored for reliability and validity – a requirement of the examining boards. Once a piece of work has been submitted by a student it is then graded. The type of grading depends on the qualification, with evaluation for GNVQ programmes arguably taking the longest, following a rigid and laborious procedure. This has been recognized and is currently under review by educational committees. Grades then need to be recorded and tracked on a paperwork system which varies from one examination board to another.

Key issues

Teachers do not always have the benefit of information processing. This may mean that they have to keep records manually when technology would be more efficient and effective. An example of this is the registration system where the teacher calls out the name of each student and marks them absent or present. Is this really necessary? In the technological age we now live in, a swipe system, or 'logging on', would remove a manual task, speedily analyse data and could produce letters to parents advising them of their child's attendance. A further use of information technology could be to advise examination boards directly of results without going through the manual task of completing forms periodically.

In further education, 'quality' files need to be maintained for each course. These files contain a wealth of course information including student details, grades, examination reports and staffing qualifications. Much of this work is repetitive, produced in different formats to those who request it. This includes the Further Education Funding Council, examination boards, auditors and college management.

Complex recording systems exist for assessment: with a wide number of examination boards, students on one course may sit exams for a number of examiners. The system of recording is unique to the board in question and the burden of recording in a variety of formats is increased.

The time taken to complete administrative duties detracts from the teaching time given to students.

Conclusion

From the above, we may conclude that:

▌ Information processing is not used effectively.
▌ Students suffer from reduced teaching and assessment time.
▌ Teachers have increased administrative duties, detracting from their original desire to teach.
▌ Data provision lacks computability.
▌ Numerous meetings are held to discuss changes and developments in assessment and other operating systems.
▌ Morale may be low due to the repetitive nature of the administrative burden.
▌ Teachers and lecturers have less time for preparation and marking.

■ Support personnel have to respond to the administrative requirements of a live organization within a rapidly changing environment.

Exchange programmes

Large numbers of people come to Britain from other countries to study, and British people work and train overseas. The British aid programme encourages links between educational institutions in Britain and developing countries. Alongside this, there has been an expansion of interest in European studies and languages, with exchanges of teachers, school children and students taking place.

How do they affect teachers?

The following may increase stress and need to be considered:

■ increased administration time to develop links and opportunities;
■ students have additional needs whilst away from home;
■ language barriers to learning;
■ 'home' students may be discouraged by a language barrier during academic work.

Role conflict and role ambiguity

It is probable that role conflict and role ambiguity are often the causal effects of increased levels of stress in education. Role conflict can be defined as taking into consideration all aspects of a job and the demands of an organization and having to make choices which may conflict with the personal beliefs of an individual. Role ambiguity is when an individual has a lack of clear and consistent information regarding personal goals, responsibilities, rights and duties and how best they can be carried out. This ambiguity often creates a sense of conflict, anger and ultimately discouragement. This problem arises as a result of factors such as lack of clarity about the scope and responsibilities of the job, uncertainty about what colleagues expect of them, lack of information required to perform tasks adequately and doubt about the career opportunities available. Doubts and uncertainties about roles increase during periods of personal and organizational change.

Many teachers report having a sense of role conflict when inappropriate, incompatible and inconsistent demands are placed on them. When two or more sets of these inconsistent role behaviours are experienced by an individual, role conflict results. When the teacher cannot reconcile inconsistencies between these sets of expected role behaviours, they experience conflict. Firstly, they are expected to provide quality education for their students while they do not have at their disposal the best teaching materials. Secondly, they are held responsible for handling the discipline problems in their classes while they are not given the authority to do so. The great promise of teaching, the reward of personal satisfaction and sense of accomplishment, is increasingly being unfulfilled. The joy of helping others grow and watching them mature is dampened, even destroyed, by the growing tensions, stultifying conditions and unrealistic demands on the profession and teachers. The degenerating morale of teachers is a reflection of the stressful conditions of work and the disillusionment.

When teachers have pastoral care responsibilities and a full teaching load, these demands lead to stress. Role conflict also exists as teachers are aware of the expectations of parents, school governors, the government, the media, the funding bodies and inspectors.

Teachers are trained to provide quality education for their students. They enter the profession with excitement in sharing their knowledge with others. After a short while, they find that they are not being encouraged to use the teaching methods they learnt were best for students. Curriculum materials are often not available. Administrative constraints, disruptive pupils, overcrowded classes and often poor physical facilities prevent them from reaching the goals they once had.

Key issues

The increasing pace of organizational and curricular changes in schools and colleges has resulted in major problems of role ambiguity and role conflict for staff. Many find that the job they came in to do – teach – is not the same any more. Many feel that their roles have changed so much that their loyalties are less strong as the underpinning values of their professionalism. There are strong recommendations from government, parents, media, industry and the funding bodies that the predominant roles are those of marketplace economics, cost effectiveness, cost-cutting, profit and increased efficiency. The 90s theme is value for money with a free-market economy between colleges in an open enrolment situation, especially where funding is directly related to student numbers. These developments are an anathema to teachers whose earlier professional experience was gained in a very different culture. Role conflict in education is brought about through ever-changing demands and an atmosphere of ambiguity. Teachers and lecturers commonly have to take on several of the following activities, frequently changing their 'hat' according to the situation. Conflicts arise due to lack of time to prepare for these roles and, in many cases, lack of support:

- lecturer;
- counsellor;
- salesperson;
- appraiser;
- administrator;
- friend;
- programme manager;
- supervisor;
- confidant;
- advisor;
- course developer;
- mentor.

Conclusion

The following may increase levels of stress and need to be considered:

- Teachers may not always have clear job descriptions.
- Goals and targets are not always realistic.
- Teachers have to develop a variety of personal skills.
- Some students need additional pastoral care.
- There may be conflict between lecturers through ambiguity and lack of direction.
- Lack of time prevents many roles from being effectively managed.
- 'Change' may not always be communicated.
- Levels of authority, responsibility and accountability are often unclear.

PART 3
How the main education sectors differ

Primary and secondary schools

In 1988 a new Education Act was passed by the government. It empowered school governors to decide how school budgets should be spent, including the number of staff, staff selection and appointment, pay policies, discipline and grievance procedures. The Act set up the National Curriculum and a system of testing students at four key stages.

The Education Act of 1992 changed the inspection of schools and set up the Office for Standards in Education, OFSTED. Its role is to inspect schools every four years. The main focus of the inspection is the quality of teaching and learning in classrooms.

The 1993 Education Act set up the School Curriculum and Assessment Authority. Among other things, this empowered the Secretary of State for Education to take over school management in schools seen to be failing.

The National Curriculum consists of core subjects which are compulsory for 5–16 year olds, together with foundation subjects which are studied up to the age of 14. In England, the core subjects are English, mathematics and science. Foundation subjects are technology, history, geography, music, art and physical education. At secondary school level, a modern language is also included.

Following a thorough review in 1994, a revised National Curriculum was introduced for 5–14 year olds. The idea was to release more time outside the statutory curriculum and to give teachers more scope to use their professional discretion.

National testing and assessment of pupils' performance at the ages of 7, 11 and 14 is confined to the core subjects. All 11- and 14-year-olds are tested in the three areas, whereas at 7 they are tested in English and maths only. The intention of the tests is to see whether pupils have reached National Curriculum learning targets.

League tables

These were introduced in the latter half of the 1990s as a per-formance indicator. Schools were graded according to their results and this enabled parents of current and prospective pupils to identify the schools doing well from those schools achieving poor results. These results are published in national newspapers. Many schools use their local paper as a forum to highlight their success and at the same time dismiss any weak-nesses or suggest ongoing strategies for improvement. While private schools do not have to publish their results, most do because they know that it will show them in a good light and act as a good advertisement.

Changes and the effects on teachers

Many experienced teachers left the profession during these developments because:

- lack of communication meant that teachers were unsure of the future;
- they felt that they wouldn't be able to cope with the new National Curriculum;
- they felt change had not been discussed and implemented effectively;
- the new workload removed them from their intended role, that of teaching pupils;
- administration and record-keeping meant that they were employed as administrators as much as teachers;
- the only way to gain promotion was through a management spine which removed them from the classroom.

Those continuing to teach noted that their workload increased because of the level of paperwork and administration they had to do in addition to their teaching load. Instead of teaching pupils, marking and preparing work as in the past, they had new roles and responsibilities.

Higher education

Higher education provides education at undergraduate level (eg to BA or BSc) and post-graduate level (MA, MBA, MSc or higher). Students have different levels of needs according to whether they are studying on a full- or part-time basis.

Full-time students generally follow-on through the education system. Part-time students often have full-time jobs and study during evenings and at weekends.

Full-time students

Many full-time students work on a part-time basis in order to support themselves financially. Changes in government policy regarding financial support mean that many students are constantly in debt and so need employment. This may mean that their university work suffers. This affects the lecturer because:

▌ students may take time off from university to earn more money;
▌ students may fall behind with their work;
▌ students may be too tired to study to their full potential;
▌ students may have other personal problems affecting their ability.

Part-time students

Most part-time students work on a full-time basis. When they attend a university programme they often:

▌ have little or no financial support from their employer;
▌ have little or no support in 'time' from their employer;
▌ are tired because they are at work all day;
▌ have a great deal of knowledge to bring to the class which may detract from the purpose;
▌ expect much support from the lecturer because they have paid a great deal of money to the university.

While there have been some changes within the higher education sector, and there is evidence of more to come (likely to be similar to those in further education), most of the changes in post-16 education have so far been within further education.

Further Education

A survey by the National Association of Teachers in Further and Higher Education (NATFHE, 1997) at Manchester Metropolitan University shows that stress is continuing to rise. Since colleges became self-governed and financed through the Further Education Funding Council (Incorporation), stress levels have risen dramatically while staff morale has plummeted. Of those who responded, 65 per cent reported increased stress levels compared to a previous survey and 97 per cent experienced some kind of stress. The major causes of stress were identified as time pressures, work overload, poor communication, low participation in decision-making, lack of control over the pacing of work, poor pay and poor job environment.

Further education operates in a diverse and complex environment. Historically routine in many areas, such as holidays, examinations and methods of teaching, the process, as a result of government changes, market forces and competition, is rapidly changing. Flexibility has been encouraged, and the academic year is expanding from its former 36 weeks to an almost year-round programme. Incorporation, a move towards independence from local authority, the establishment of self-managed business centres to generate further income and an increase in qualifications and awarding bodies have increased the number of environmental sectors. While the degree of routine was fairly clear, the introduction of industry-led courses at times formerly alien to colleges, eg at weekends and over summer months, and the introduction of roll-on roll-off programmes, has altered the environment from static to dynamic.

Lecturers have been faced with new 'flexible' contracts with increased hours, less holidays and generally poorer conditions. Registers are used to calculate teaching hours in each year, affecting pay and holiday entitlement. Redundancies are sought in many colleges. Morale is often low. As a result of past practice, education operates in a hostile environment. The dilemma facing the general public is the view that while supporting and encouraging the need for education, academic staff have had an easy time in the past with extended holiday periods and a short working week. Very few are aware of weekday and weekend marking and preparation sessions. To this end, few are sympathetic with regard to pay claims, new 'flexible' contracts and stressful situations.

In March 1991 the government announced the intention to remove colleges of further education and sixth-form colleges from the control of local authorities to form a new sector for the provision of post-16 education and training. Incorporation finally happened on 1 April 1973 – known as 'Vesting Day', when staff, land and other assets were transferred from local education authorities to corporations, ie colleges.

Until 1 April 1993, the further education sector was maintained by local authorities. Their responsibilities included employment, payroll, staff welfare, premises supervision and maintenance, and the operational financial systems generating income. Incorporation has divorced the management of colleges from local authorities and presented each college management team with the responsibilities of a live organization. This has created a number of new operational sectors including a human resource department, premises and maintenance, management information systems and finance. Colleges are now funded in the main by the Further Education Funding Council which, as paymaster, also acts in an inspection role to maintain a quality provision.

The impact of the FEFC

The Further Education Funding Council (FEFC) was set up under the Further and Higher Education Act 1992 to ensure that there are sufficient and adequate further education facilities throughout England. It does so mainly through funding further and sixth-form education institutions together with those universities which provide further education courses. The Council has a number of specific legal duties including:

1. ensuring that there are sufficient further education opportunities for young people and adults in every part of England and Wales;
2. ensuring that the needs of students with learning difficulties and/or disabilities are met;
3. making arrangements to assess the quality of further education funded by the Council;
4. monitoring the availability of further education opportunities by analysing college strategic plans;
5. employing inspectors to ensure the quality of provision;
6. reporting on a national basis on specific curriculum areas and qualifications.

It does all of the above by advising the Secretary of State for education on the financial needs of the further education sector in England, deciding on how recurrent and capital funds will be allocated, allocating and monitoring funds.

The Council receives funds on an annual basis from the Department for Education and Employment as part of the public expenditure settlement agreed by parliament. It then allocates funds to a wide range of vocational and academic qualifications in one of two methods – recurrent funds and capital funds. Within recurrent funding, the largest element is teaching and support staff salaries, while capital funds assist colleges with the costs of capital equipment and the repair and construction of buildings. Through its recurrent funding methodology, the Council allocates £3.2 billion a year (1999 figure) to 452 further education and sixth-form colleges, 48 universities and higher education colleges and over 350 other institutions. Each college forwards its strategic plan annually to the FEFC. This sets out its objectives. Funds are allocated to support the plan as follows:

1. All institutions funded by the Council automatically receive a percentage, currently 90 per cent, of the previous year's funding. This is known as the core funding.
2. Institutions then apply for funding above the core by applying for additional 'funding units'.

To provide a common measure for funding purposes, the Council has adopted the concept of funding units rather than actual student enrolments. Each student attracts a number of funding units for the college, the precise number depending on the course. The college also earns units for pre-enrolment advice and guidance and for making a learner agreement with each student which sets out the education, training and support the college will provide. Additional funding units are available for supporting students with learning difficulties and special needs. The provision of an average-sized college amounts to around 400,000 units. The largest college has 1.6 million units.

In accord with most businesses in the public sector, further education is within tight controls for meeting targets. For a college to gain maximum funding, students need to pass through the three census points of 1 November, 1 February and 15 May of each academic year. If they then successfully complete their course, the total amount of their funding is allowed. For example:

If a full-time student is enrolled for a year	135 units
If withdrawn before 1 November	0 units
If withdrawn after 1 November	47 units
If withdrawn after 1 February	86 units
If withdrawn after 15 May	125 units
If successful	10 units

Clearly the impact of the funding methodology is to increase and retain the students in order to make the most of the funding available.

Conclusions

∎ Colleges are self-managed, live organizations responsible for their own financial destiny through budgetary control, funded by the FEFC.
∎ They are responsible for staffing, welfare, premises and maintenance and the other operational factors of a live organization, which were previously dealt with by local authorities.
∎ Lecturers are employed on conditions less favourable than those adopted in the past.

■ Colleges are funded to their maximum allocation when students pass through three census points and are successful.
■ Course tutors are 'encouraged' to make allowances for students in order to achieve maximum funding – behaviour and ability.
■ Learning agreements to ensure funding are complex and deduct from teaching time.
■ Requirements for the completion of a learning agreement are often repeated from a student's application form and entry/induction processes.
■ Courses vary in funding 'richness'.

Education reports

Government white papers in 1994 heralded the way for a series of four reports for the development of education which have been officially accepted. Each report recommends a series of changes which lead to additional demands on the service providers.

Following publication of the reports, a series of targets were set encompassing many changes in the education sector. These targets and their implications are individually detailed below, but all are consistent with the government's policy document on Lifetime Learning which emphasizes:

■ the importance of flexible delivery;
■ the need for courses to be tailored to meet the particular groups of learners;
■ the need to promote new attitudes to learning and bring back those who no longer see learning as relevant;
■ participation.

Developments in the structure of education bring about changes not only for the learner, but also for the education provider. Each report focuses on a different aspect of the education sector and together they bring about change on a mammoth scale. Funding, as a result of student success, will depend on schools and colleges getting to grips with each report and implementing its recommendations. The burden of these changes, especially at operational level, will undoubtedly add to teacher stress.

The Dearing Report

One of the major issues highlighted by the Dearing Report, published in March 1996, was that there were too many alternative qualifications available at differing levels by different examining boards. Consequently, employers and learners were confused by the options available. The intention of the Dearing Report was to tame the diversity of over 1,600 qualifications. Some examination boards were amalgamated.

NCVQ + SCAA merged from September 1997 to form QNCA.
RSAEB has a collaborative agreement with UCLES.
City and Guilds has a collaborative agreement with NEAB, AEB and WJEC.
BTEC has merged with ULEAC to form EDEXCEL.

This leaves a further 145 NVQ awarding bodies!

The Beaumont Report

Key recommendations of the Beaumont Report were as follows:

- ministers are asked to confirm that National Vocational Qualifications (NVQ) are here to stay and have a place in the development of educational standards;
- all standards for NVQs and SVQs should spell out relevant core skills for the job;
- plain English (or Welsh) must be used in all documents;
- all organizations should remove unnecessary bureaucracy;
- new guidance and examples of best practice should be given on assessment, the use of portfolios and simulation;
- better marketing is needed to help implement NVQs more widely;
- all traditional qualifications competing with the NVQ framework should be made compatible with the NVQ framework.

Learning Works – The Kennedy Report

An independent committee, chaired by barrister Helena Kennedy QC, called on the government to put further education at the heart of the post-16 agenda and urged a dramatic shift in policy to focus on people who left school with little or no qualifications. The final report 'Learning Works' argued that widening participation in post-school education is key to economic prosperity for both the nation and individuals and that further education is a weapon against poverty which will create a more cohesive society.

The report suggests that while colleges have been successful in recruiting increasing numbers to courses, they have been less successful in the recruitment of those who have not usually been present in further education. These groups of people include:

- people without qualifications;
- unemployed people;
- some groups of women, such as those in low income groups and those who are single parents;
- some groups of men, including white men in low income groups;
- some minority ethnic groups, including refugees;
- those over 50 years old;
- people with literacy and/or numeracy difficulties;
- people with learning difficulties and/or disabilities from minority ethnic groups;
- people with profound and/or multiple disabilities;
- adults with mental illness;
- young people with emotional and behavioural difficulties;
- ex-offenders;
- part-time and temporary workers;
- unskilled manual workers.

Impact of educational reports on teaching staff

The following table identifies the key issues within each report and the subsequent effect on lecturers.

Table 3.4 Educational reports

Key issues	Impact
Capey Report	
Development of exemplar material and standard assignments for key skills	Reduces burden on teaching staff to develop their own material, 'reinventing the wheel'
Joint mandatory test production from City and Guilds, BTEC/Edexcel, and RSA.	Standard style of written tests
One externally set assignment	Provides a national standard
Development of a more 'user friendly' grading system	Reduces the burden of excessive marking, grading and assessment
Language review	Provides for a more easily understood requirement
Dearing Report	
Co-ordination of cross-curricular teams	Meeting time
Knowledge of different assessment arrangements eg lecturers will need to have a knowledge of GNVQ assessment and 'A' level and vice versa	Staff development requirement at the expense of other issues eg pastoral care
Dramatic changes in further education provision	Frequent changes represent a belief of lack of understanding and belief with the original concept – and future situations
New delivery models for one- and two-year programmes, timetabling for breadth, modularization and curriculum rather than subject-based teams	Shifting away from subject-based programmes
Possible reduced contact time within each programme and an increase in hours for generic issues	Less lecturer input
Linking pathways across the programmes	Staff development need
New delivery models	Developing new programmes
Streamlining the regulatory and awarding bodies – mergers and collaboration to provide a new standardized approach	Less choice of exam boards

Beaumont Report

Confirmation of the continued use of NVQs	End to the confusion about future of NVQs as a competence-based qualification framework
Removal of bureaucratic system for assessment	Beneficial approach in the long term. Short-term changes represent staff development
Guidance on best practice	Benefits colleges and provides for a standard approach
Plain English to be used in NVQ documentation	Benefits lecturers and students
All traditional qualifications competing with the NVQ framework to be made compatible with the NVQ framework	Changes to course content and provision

Kennedy Report

'Widening Participation' encompasses those not from a mainstream educational route	Staff development requirement. Lecturers need to be retrained to deal with the needs of each type of group eg over 50s or those with literacy/numeracy difficulties
Extended programmes to identify with different cultures	Staff development requirement to understand various cultures
Generate a needs-based education system together with an outcome-based system	College funding currently depends on market forces
Develop an outreach programme eg sites within the community, such as snooker halls and pubs	Staff travelling time
Creatively design educational packages for widening participation groups	Extra pressures to design new packages away from traditional methods
Provide education at times suitable for special needs groups	Pressures of dealing with mainstream and special needs groups
Develop funding for a student to be unit rich	Encouraging colleges to seek students from outside mainstream groups.
Alteration in funding methodology to suit those not from mainstream groups	Pressures of dealing with benefit claimants
Off-site education	Varying resources

Figure 3.1 Causes of stress in education

		Organizational issues eg Resources Facilities Rules		
Customer status factors		Structure Culture Objectives		Service provision management
		⇩		
Student stressors	⇨	*Physiological*	⇦	Funding
eg		*and*	⇦	Role ambiguity
behaviour	⇨	*psychological*	⇦	Communication
role conflict	⇨	*outcomes*	⇦	Job security
		⇧		

Personal capacity factors
Unexplained

Unwarranted

External

Occasional...extreme

Without communication

Unreasoned

Demanding

Apparently unnecessary

Chapter conclusion

The above figure acts as a conclusion to this chapter in that it draws together all the issues that may increase negative stress for the teacher and result in the physiological or psychological outcomes as detailed in Chapter 2. There are four main areas to consider and these are:

1. *Organizational issues* include the factors that are wholly contributed to the organization such as the rules set in place by the management, organizational culture, adequate facilities and resources.
2. *Customer status factors* where the customers are the students. They bring with them a range of issues such as personal conduct or problems which intrude on the aims and objectives of the lesson.
3. *Service provision management* covers a wide area of internal and external influences, all leading to the possibility of negative stress.
4. *Personal capacity factors* are the final link. Chapter 2 identified that every person has a personal threshold or capacity. When this capacity is overloaded, healthy pressure or positive stress becomes a negative issue. Many of the contributory factors are the result of a lack of organizational systems needed to communicate new practices and procedures. Consequently, the teacher is left with a feeling of uncertainty and a lack of understanding as to why the changes were made. With teaching being a paradigm (see Chapter 1), the need for change has to be clearly communicated to those involved.

4 *The law*

Chapter goals

This chapter identifies some of the legal issues relating to a teacher at work. These include:

- the duties of employers and other people you work with;
- treatment of staff;
- grievance and enforcement.

Perception and the law

The understanding of occupational stress is very much one of self-perception. The degree to which an employee is stressed, either through employment or personal life, is subjective. Measurement only comes in part from the physical symptoms which may, or may not, be identified. Consequently, there are no specific employment laws relating to stress. Employers, however, have a duty of care towards their employees, and the actions of the latter, which may be a stress-related consequence, fall within the scope of existing employment legislation.

The Conservative government of 1992–97 abandoned publication of a stress guide for employers that suggested that workers working more than 48 hours a week were twice as likely to develop serious illness. The Department of Health claimed that the conclusion was based on research more than 20 years old and that recent evidence did not support the same findings.

The 1990 Labour Force survey estimated that 183,000 people in England and Wales believed that they had work-related stress, depression or anxiety and that 105,000 of these believed the condition was caused by, rather than made worse by, work. This group of conditions represented the second most frequently reported after musculoskeletal problems within the survey. Analysis identified some occupational groups which rated significantly above average, including teachers, professionals and other education and welfare workers.

In 1995 a survey by the Health and Safety Executive identified that 37,000 teachers suffered from stress, anxiety or depression. A further survey sponsored by the *Times Educational Supplement* in 1997 suggested that almost 40 per cent of teachers who resigned their jobs did so because of a stress-related problem.

The difficulty with the simple self-reporting or work-related psychological disorders employed by these surveys lies in interpreting precisely what is being reported. Subjects' understanding of stress, such as perceived stigma or lack of recognition, may influence reporting of this condition and such factors could be related to occupational group or social class. Furthermore, the perception of suffering occupational stress may underlie the reporting of some other conditions such as stomach upset.

Employment legislation

Under current legislation, an employer has a duty to take reasonable care of an employee's physical well-being and mental health. In education, this includes ensuring that unacceptable levels of negative stress are not placed on a teacher. Case law states that an employer must take reasonable care for the safety of employees by providing:

▮ competent fellow employees;
▮ a reasonably safe system of work;
▮ reasonably safe equipment.

The law also recognizes that there must be trust and confidence between employer and employee. Consequently, an employer must not do anything that will unfairly single out, humiliate or harass a teacher. If this happens, the employee may be entitled to a claim for constructive dismissal on the grounds of the employer's unreasonable behaviour.

The behaviour of other teachers and pupils

The employer's duty to provide a safe system of work extends to the behaviour of pupils and colleagues. A school has a responsibility to maintain codes of discipline and, while it cannot be liable in the first instance for the unruly or dangerous behaviour of others, it may be found to be liable if the actions are repeated. An example could be that if a school is aware of a pupil, or member of staff, who has been disruptive and possibly dangerous to the welfare of others, steps should be taken to avert a repeat of such behaviour.

A further issue is that of bullying. Most people would assume that this would take the form of pupils bullying each other. This is not always the case and many teachers find themselves being harassed by colleagues and managers, especially when schools are under pressure to achieve better results. Parents may also be over critical of methods used by the classroom teacher, resulting in a teacher feeling bullied.

The important issue is that schools and colleges need to have a clear strategy for dealing with stress and bullying, dealing with it effectively through a grievance procedure.

Health and Safety at Work Act 1974

There is no specific legislation on controlling stress at work as not enough is known to set standards or requirements. However, employers have a duty of care to their employees under the Health and Safety at Work Act 1974 to ensure that, so far as is reasonably practicable, their workplaces are safe and healthy. Employers have taken very good care to ensure that the risk of physical danger to their employees is minimal. Eye tests for computer operators and risk assessments for physical danger are the main thrust of their approach. However, many employers still do not understand the multitude of problems that may be out of sight – the mental and other problems caused by stressful situations.

Management of Health and Safety Regulations

Under the Management of Health and Safety Regulations 1993 employers are obliged to assess the nature and scale of risks to health in their workplace and base their control methods on it. Most employers have in place a series of risk assessments in regard to the *physical* health and safety aspects but fail to carry out risk assessments for stress based on issues such as workload, responsibility, resources and so on.

The Workplace (Health, Safety and Welfare) Regulations 1992

These regulations make it compulsory for an employer to:

■ maintain the workplace and equipment in an efficient state;
■ ensure safe access to the premises;
■ ensure all glazings meet safety standards;
■ provide drinking water;
■ provide rest rooms.

Enforcing the law

The Health and Safety Executive (HSE) has the authority to prosecute employers who fail in their duty with regard to health and safety issues. Mostly they investigate following accidents at the workplace. The HSE has published guidelines on work-related stress and has urged employers to take the issue seriously and be understanding towards staff who show signs of wilting under pressure. The guidelines are not binding on employers. However, there is an increasing legal element that employers need to be aware of and managers should be:

▌ clear about company policy and objectives;
▌ able to communicate fully with their staff;
▌ able to offer opportunities for involvement in planning and organization.

A key element in recent cases has been that the employer should anticipate that the employee might experience adverse effects from his or her work. The scale of work-related stress in employment is to be addressed in a new research project commissioned by the government. A team of psychologists aims to distinguish stress caused by work from that caused by other factors. It will then assess the effects of stress on the health of the population.

Legal action

An employee who resigns from his or her job as a result of negative stress may feel unable to continue because of the actions of the employer. To gain compensation they have to prove, at an industrial tribunal, that the employer's behaviour constituted constructive dismissal.

Employees who have suffered negative stress can, if they wish, make a claim for compensation. It is a civil issue and can be actioned through the civil courts. Like constructive dismissal, it is up to the employee to prove that he or she suffered as a result of the employer's actions. The employee has to prove that there was foreseeable damage to health. In other words, if the employer realizes that there is stress in the workplace and does nothing to improve the situation, and consequently the health of the employee suffers as a result of negative stress, the employer may be liable.

In both cases, it is up to the employee to prove the case and provide evidence. Successful cases have provided the following types of evidence:

▌ job descriptions;
▌ person specifications;
▌ evidence of training and development;
▌ doctors/welfare input;
▌ minutes of meetings with managers;
▌ appraisal interview notes;
▌ reports of disciplinary meetings, procedures and actions;
▌ support given to date;
▌ advice/support given to all staff.

The burden of proof is very much on the employee who, for this reason, has to be fully prepared. The nature of negative stress, as detailed in Chapter 2, suggests that it may depend on a person's personality and physical makeup. The employer, in defence, may well argue that the stress is a personal issue, outside the control of the working environment, or that the *depth* of the negativity is solely attributable to the personality of the employee and consequently will not admit liability. The overwhelming issue here, though, is that if a teacher is off work for a stress-related problem or has made management aware of an ongoing problem, and no action has been taken to remedy the situation, the employer may be seen to be liable.

Sick building syndrome

The term sick building syndrome (SBS) refers to a range of relatively minor illnesses which can be caused by the indoor environment. SBS can be identified by the prevalence of symptoms in a building being greater than expected and by the tendency for them to disappear away from the building. No single specific cause has been identified, but factors which could be implicated include air-conditioning, poor lighting, poor heating, air pollution and noise. Typical symptoms include tiredness, irritation, anxiety, dry skin and nasal problems. Because these problems are common in the general population, and for the most part not serious, they are rarely reported to a doctor. Doctors cannot with any certainty connect the symptoms to conditions at work and therefore it is difficult to quantify the numbers affected.

While many of the symptoms associated with SBS are thought to be stress related, the employer also has a duty to ensure that the symptoms do not stem from a failure to impose adequate health and safety regulations.

Conclusion

While stress at work may not be covered by a specific law, issues are included in employment and health and safety legislation.

Two-thirds of trade union safety representatives believe stress has become the biggest health hazard employees face at work, according to a Trades Union Congress report published on 7 October 1996. It says that stress has turned into 'the new industrial epidemic'.

Ill health resulting from stress caused at work has to be treated in the same way as ill health due to other physical conditions present in the workplace. This means that employers have a legal duty to take reasonable care to ensure that health is not placed at risk through excessive and sustained levels of stress arising from the way in which the work is organized.

Employers should bear stress in mind when assessing possible health hazards in their workplaces. Eliminating unnecessary stress from work will keep employees fit and healthy and ensure the work environment is safe yet competitive.

If remedies are not taken to avoid stress or bullying, an employer may be found to be liable.

5 *Management issues to reduce stress in teaching*

Chapter goals

The purpose of this chapter is to provide some sort of direction to the management of education and to those who are managers and teachers. It looks at:

▌ the benefits of reducing the impact of stress;
▌ organizational systems, resources and influences;
▌ a stress checklist;
▌ management qualities.

While an individual can lessen the stressors through a series of health initiatives, as detailed in Chapter 7, it is not feasible or likely that an individual will be able to develop an extensive and all encompassing support system without recognition and support from those they work with. Nevertheless, it is important that both managers and teachers at the operational level appreciate the possible frameworks that can help reduce stress.

The systems developed need to be a long-term commitment, reinforced periodically, in order to be successful. Like other health problems it is all too easy to say, 'I have tried that, and yes it did work, but then it stopped working'. Stress is a long-term problem, like long-term illnesses. There are no immediate cures, and some treatments lessen the symptoms only as long as the treatment is being taken. Similarly, like antibiotics, you have to take the full course of medicine to avoid a recurrence. Negative stress reduction is a lifestyle change. The difference between this and a diet is that at work you are part of a team, controlling the problem together. It needs to be a joint commitment.

The first step after realizing that there is a problem is to ask questions:

▌ What are the benefits to change?
▌ What will be different if the problem is resolved?
▌ Who will be affected by change?
▌ Is there a need for altruism within employment?
▌ Is it realized that without caring there can be no quality?

Stress from all directions

We have already seen that exposure to the heavy pressures within an occupation is responsible for the development of behavioural, emotional, mental and physical reactions when the pressures are significantly greater than the coping skills available. Research has shown that teachers have a variety of responses to these additional pressures, ranging from finding a new zest for teaching to developing a greater range of negative feelings.

Much has been written about how to cope more effectively with stress. Ideas include diet, exercise, meditation and relaxation. One major problem with this advice is that often no attempt is made to help people relate their needs to the recommendations. Books and materials on stress often talk of pampering yourself, going to a health farm and other self-indulgences. These can work, but they are not a long-term answer – they simply relieve the symptom. They are rarely related to the work issues and it is these that cause the problem. The long-term solution lies with a radical and alternative strategy.

Identify where the stress is coming from

Chapter 3 looked at the possible causes of negative stress. Remedies , like medicine, only work when they are applied to the problem. It is therefore important to identify the source. Research suggests the following six ground rules for learning how to reduce stress:

1. Accept the possibility of the existence of stress in colleagues and self.
2. Learn to understand what stress is.
3. Begin to tackle the problem by identifying the pressures from change, role conflict, poor working conditions and pupil behaviour.
4. Learn to recognize personal reactions to pressure – for example, in personal behaviour and body language, emotions, thinking, and physical reactions and change.
5. Identify coping strategies inside and outside work.
6. Develop stress reduction training programmes at individual/section/department/school/college/university level for the development of resources to reduce stress.

Benefits of change

Until recently it was thought that stress was simply a result of a person's ability to cope. This is no longer always applicable, as stress is more often than not an issue for the organization and its environment. Changing the organization in order to actively manage, and in the long term to reduce stress, will result in changes that benefit:

▌ the student;
▌ the parent;
▌ the school, college or university;
▌ education management and education managers;
▌ the country and its developing economy (the value of the workforce).

Change may result in:

1. improved learning;
2. less waste of time;

3. higher standards;
4. parental support;
5. quality issues and control;
6. improved resources for industry;
7. higher success factors;
8. less negative stress;
9. less confusion;
10. no double standards;
11. standard products;
12. more time for action learning.

Key issues

Teachers usually have many recommendations for the improvement of the management and administration of schools and colleges and the services provided by organizations within their environment. Their main proposals may include:

■ improved physical resources;
■ improved staff selection techniques;
■ more effective job induction;
■ an effective communication system;
■ using information technology and processing for competitive advantage;
■ improved industrial relations;
■ greater realization and understanding for direct employees;
■ a holistic competitive strategy;
■ development of enhanced reward and remuneration programmes;
■ staff development in time management and assertiveness.

An organizational strategy for management

There are three identifiable areas which, when acted upon concurrently, lessen the causes and effects of stress in education. They are:

1. organization systems;
2. organization resources;
3. organization influence.

Organization systems

Many organizations often do not fully appreciate or act on the implications of educational changes and developments until the implications are forced upon them. It is common to deal with problems as they arise and not with the issues that may pre-empt the problem. The development of a proactive rather than a reactive approach provides a number of benefits:

∎ the ability to head off problems;
∎ calculating a value with all the facts;
∎ providing information on what's coming;
∎ getting to the source of a problem;
∎ creating time;
∎ developing new initiatives;
∎ achieving and feeling successful.

The alternative reactive strategy pours out the negative issues of:

∎ firefighting;
∎ 'flying by the seat of pants';
∎ lack of feeling of success;
∎ being overwhelmed;
∎ little satisfaction.

Student behaviour and Communications are two systems within an educational environment that the case studies in Chapter 8 reveal as the main contributors to negative stress. While not exhaustive, here are some suggestions for improving the management of these areas:

Student behaviour

The following recommendations will ease some of the problems in this domain:

1. Establish a working party to review codes for student behaviour. This should include staff and students. Once accepted, a fully operational and implemented disciplinary system should be re-introduced.
2. Given the security problems at schools, colleges and universities worldwide, a swipe card system should be introduced where possible, enforcing students without identification to be excluded from the main buildings, IT facilities, canteen, library and common areas. This has a dual purpose – keeping out people who are not students and for use as a library card or similar token.
3. Students who have withdrawn either through their personal choice or for other reasons should be removed from the access system of swipe card entry.
4. Some colleges and universities have security guards. The idea is that they are qualified to deal with problems as they occur. Unfortunately, some security personnel have little or no formal training and may exacerbate problems. In line with government policy initiatives for door personnel at nightclubs, it is worth considering similar training.
5. Standard letters to be used as part of a disciplinary procedure.
6. All members of the teaching and lecturing staff to implement, action and enforce accepted codes of conduct.
7. Staff themselves to act within the parameters of codes of conduct and industry-led standards of behaviour.

Communications

The following recommendations will ease problems in this domain:

1. Standardize as far as possible formal communication procedures across departments within a school or college to ensure equality and fairness.
2. Cultivate good listening techniques and encourage feedback.
3. Review and improve existing communication strategies or systems.
4. Encourage team building in formal and informal groups.
5. Use a suggestion box to encourage individuals and teams.

6. Develop an open door policy.
7. Urge open discussion leading to sensible changes.
8. Provide clear guidelines.
9. When guidelines are changed, provide effective means of communicating that previous methods are no longer operational.
10. Communicate fully all changes in simple terms.
11. Lay down clear procedures.
12. Recognize quality work and good communication and praise when appropriate.
13. As the ultimate goal, develop an extensive and responsive communication system to pre-empt the rumour factory status found in most schools, colleges and universities.

Organization resources

Notwithstanding financial constraints, there has to be some recognition that quality resources are paramount for the delivery of a quality product or service in education. The following four resources need to be considered by education managers:

Staff

Distrust of management ensures lower morale and productivity. Lack of praise and recognition or poor communications result in demotivation.

Students

One of the problems in this area is that college students on full-time courses only have 15 hours of study each week. For many, this means that they are bored, a state bringing about less enthusiasm and interest. Making the most of funding methodology by adding additional short courses in the same vocational area may generate a greater level of interest.

Equipment

Equipment needs to be more effectively controlled to avoid wastage. Give people responsibility for their equipment.

Accommodation

Upgrade staff accommodation. Teachers and lecturers note the amount of money spent on indirect issues, and feel aggrieved at working in cramped conditions. Provide all necessary resources to ensure they have the right tools for providing a quality product. In an ideal world, where a school or college is purpose built, this problem will be tackled at the design stage.

Organization influence

Many of the stressors encountered by those employed in education are the result of outside agencies, such as the government, the funding councils and examination bodies. The management of schools and colleges, both as individual institutions and together, have a collective voice which they should use to impress upon outside organizations that stress exists in the workplace and that, by conquering it, they can improve results.

An educational organization's stress checklist

The checklist can be used to identify areas of negative stress in any of the following ways:

■ as a risk assessment exercise;
■ as a medium in preparation for change;
■ as a management tool for identifying problems;
■ as a way of identifying poor practice;
■ as a measure of staff well-being.

A manager's strategy

Managers need their own personal stress reduction strategy. They have responsibilities for implementing management policy in addition to responsibilities for the well-being of their staff. In education, most managers are also teachers who suffer from their own negative stressors in much the same way as teachers elsewhere in

Table 5.1 A stress checklist

Resources
Are teaching resources adequate?
What evidence supports this?
Are teaching staff or line managers asked to identify resource needs?
Are staff aware of their budgetary allowance?
People
How do managers identify stress?
Is stress seen as a weakness?
What support is available to people suffering from stress?
How would the relationship between teachers and managers be described?
Do colleagues/managers trust each other?
Are people paid fairly for their specialist knowledge compared with industry?
What evidence supports this?
Have managers received management training?
How are teaching managers assessed as managers?
Are staff associations and network systems encouraged?
How would you describe your relationship with your . . . colleagues?
                                                 manager?
                                                 headteacher?
How would you be able to identify if they were suffering from negative stress?
Is there a good relationship between teaching sets/teams?
Support staff
Are teaching support staff adequately trained?
Are support staff allowed to teach/train?
Is this appropriate?
Do support staff have available resources?
Are support staff supportive?

Environment
Are teachers and lecturers protected from physical danger?
Are there adequate health and safety measures in place?
Are students aware of the discipline procedures in place?
Are staff adequately trained to deal with equipment eg overhead projectors?
Are the conditions of class rooms and staff rooms adequate?
Is the layout hazardous? Overcrowded? Private? Well planned?
Are there clean rest areas and toilets?
Do teaching staff have access to food and beverages/rest areas?
What communication systems are in place for staff welfare and well-being?
The job
Does the job stimulate and motivate?
What support is given to remove negative stress?
Is the teaching load fairly distributed?
What could be done to improve student behaviour?
How could technology reduce the administration load?

Are teachers supported by their line managers?
Is there adequate training for teachers to deal with pastoral care?
Is the work load overloading?
Are teachers allowed to take all the breaks as timetabled?
Are teachers and lecturers encouraged to take their full annual leave entitlement?

Opportunities
Is there an equal opportunities policy?
Are opportunities *seen* to be fair?
Are training and staff development opportunities allocated fairly?
Are teachers supported when making training and development requests?
Is adequate teaching cover found to enable staff to develop without guilt?
Do teaching staff have to make their own cover arrangements? Is this fair?
Are training needs identified?
What stress courses are available?
Reacting to change
Is change communicated *effectively* to staff? What makes you sure?
What methods are used to ensure *all* staff have notice of change?
Is information accessible?
Are teachers aware of why the changes are taking place?
What support is provided for the changes?
Are there discussions with staff representatives on a regular basis?
Has change been thoroughly thought out and discussed before implementation?
Is further training necessary?
Students
Are students aware of the codes of conduct?
Are discipline procedures in place?
Are they fully operational?
How are the parents involved in their child's progress?
Are the parent associations well represented?
Do parents *attend* parents' evenings?
How would you describe the environment of the school/college/university from the students' perspective?

the hierarchy. They have also to implement management policy, a policy that they may have formulated with their peers.

Managers have two key reasons for aiming to reduce stress in their workforce. Firstly, they have a social duty to provide a reasonable quality of working life. Secondly, excessive stress can reduce the effectiveness of the organization through poor performance and lower job satisfaction.

Managers also need to be aware of how to ensure their own well-being, for through self knowledge they can learn techniques for problem solving among their staff. When managers are aware of the pressures they are under personally they are far better placed to be aware of the levels of stress among their staff. Likewise, managers who themselves are under pressure will often pass on the pressure to their team. An irritable or inconsistent manager may not get the best performance from their team because they will be unsure of the direction to take, unclear about what is expected of them, anxious or possibly threatened.

A manager has to be fully aware about a member of their team's behaviour in order to notice a behavioural change that might indicate stress. Clues about a person's ability to cope may be identified because of their sickness record, their non-culpable inefficiency or a disciplinary matter.

The teacher/manager might identify stress in one of their team because the teacher:

- finds it difficult to cope with a group of students when there have been no previous signs of a difficulty;
- cannot keep up with their administrative load;
- deals with a student disciplinary matter incorrectly;
- is emotional;
- has approached the manager;
- has a greater level of sickness;
- is less co-operative.

In Chapter 1 it was said that stress sometimes carries a stigma, a feeling that it is a weakness on the part of the person who is suffering. As a manager, dealing with stress is a delicate matter requiring the manager to be:

- confidential;
- fully attentive to the problem;
- sensitive and sympathetic;
- supportive.

The member of staff needs to be reassured of the above too.

What makes a manager?

In management, the manager is far more important for what he or she *is* than for what he or she knows or is able do. The manager has to be:

- enthusiastic;
- visionary;
- organized;
- persuasive;
- motivational;
- imaginative;
- able to draw upon past experience;
- able to inspire commitment;
- empathetic;
- sympathetic;
- responsible.

How you manage reflects your personal qualities, your preferences, needs, wants and motives. Your attitudes and the way that you manage will affect the way others work around you and how they perform in their jobs. There is no one way to manage effectively and each manager has to find their own way of being effective through experience and management training. Sadly, in education many managers have no formal management training, and because the systems operating when they were classroom teachers were so different to those of the present time, they may have little understanding or sympathy for the stressed teacher, or may even regard stress as a personal weakness.

Good management in this regard requires managers to be aware of the current issues which junior teachers face, and to be sympathetic to stress and effective in dealing with it.

Supporting your teachers from start to finish

Applications

One of the primary ways to reduce stress in education at its root is to ensure that the selection process for new staff is comprehensive and that the right person for the job is appointed. In most cases the selection process involves the teacher/manager who will be directly responsible for the new appointee. Frequently, however, the manager has no detailed experience of recruitment and will need advice, support and training in recruitment methods.

The following points should normally be considered when seeking to appoint the most suitable candidate:

1. What does the organization need? Carefully review the job description to ensure the job to be advertised is the same as the post needing to be filled.
2. What tasks are to be performed by the new member of staff? (Job description)
3. What sort of person is required? What skills should the appointed person possess? (Person specification)
4. Write a full and descriptive advertisement. This can be tricky but it is necessary to be accurate. Your human resources department or advisor should be in a position to offer support.
5. Send information to applicants about the job, the tasks and the type of school/college.
6. Shortlist applicants using the given criteria.
7. Interview the shortlisted candidates. Interviewers should ideally be trained in interview techniques and you should seek advice about this if you expect to interview candidates frequently.
8. Make decisions by comparing the job description and person specification to the candidates. Too many interviewers appoint because they agree on the best candidate, which may be different from suitability for the post.

Induction

The last stage of the recruitment process is often seen as induction. Induction is the introduction of a person to the work environment and doesn't usually involve training in specifics about the job, although it may identify training needs. There is a clear link between induction and labour turnover in that a person who is unsettled due to a weak induction is more likely to become stressed and leave. This will result in work overload for other members of staff while the recruitment process is repeated, as well as additional costs of advertising and additional stress for the manager involved. The process of induction is an essential way of making a new teacher more familiar with the processes and policies within the school environment. This will include learning about:

I the history of the school or college;
I the location/catchment area;
I the availability of supporting resources.

It will also include the need to understand:

I the lines of authority and responsibility for staff;
I the lines of authority/codes of conduct for pupils;
I the welfare and support systems available;
I the rules and regulations specific to the school or college;
I the methods of assessment, reporting and administration systems;
I the funding systems.

Teacher/managers should consider providing extra induction support to:

I newly qualified teachers;
I teachers returning to education;
I teachers new to a particular sector of education, such as from private to state school;
I teachers taking on senior roles for the first time.

Performance review, appraisal and staff development

Appraisal is the evaluation and judgement of a teacher's performance made in a standard and uniform manner. It should be seen as a two-way flow of communication between the manager and teacher to identify the strengths and weaknesses of a person's ability in their job. It is not a personal issue and *must* be related to the job description for that post. A good job description will clearly identify what is expected of the teacher.

An appraisal will assess past and present performance, identify skills used and those not currently utilized to the organization's advantage, identify personal growth and training needs. It may also identify areas of concern that a teacher may have as regards to coping strategies. An appraisal should *not* be used as a tool for teacher discipline. That is a separate issue.

To avoid burdening the teacher with extra stress, the manager should give plenty of notice of an appraisal interview. This will enable the teacher to think clearly and in their own time about the strengths, weaknesses, opportunities and threats that they face in their job. They may also consider the constraints they face. The most successful interviewer will be one who puts the appraisee at ease and builds a rapport or relationship. Apart from being confidential, a successful appraisal interview will be:

∎ candid;
∎ supportive;
∎ positive;
∎ constructive;
∎ productive.

In teaching, managers often need to appraise the teacher in the classroom. Care must be taken not to upset the normal classroom balance. This can be done either by becoming involved totally in the lesson or by taking a back seat. It really depends on the pupils. The teacher being appraised should be consulted, as they will normally be better placed to make a decision on this than the manager, for it is they who know the students best.

Training

If the appraisal system has identified training needs, it is important that training opportunities are made available. This will assist a teacher in career planning and development and may also lead to increased job satisfaction, reduced stress and higher levels of motivation. Training courses may include:

∎ improving teaching methods;
∎ improving technology skills;
∎ time management practices;
∎ stress management courses;
∎ management skills for promoted teachers;
∎ industrial updating;
∎ teacher training;
∎ personal development;
∎ assertiveness.

Mentoring

Many newly qualified teachers benefit from having an appointed mentor, someone with whom they can talk through problems and who may advise on their development. The mentor has the benefit of experience, but should not be seen as a hierarchical figure or manager. Through discussion and observation, mentors can motivate, praise, encourage, develop and, where necessary, criticize. It is important that the mentor is not the mentee's manager, for it may be that the intervention of a higher authority will increase the pressures and stresses on the teacher.

Welfare, support and counselling interviews

It is advantageous to provide staff with the opportunity to talk about their problems with a trained member of the human resource team or another expert, depending on the personnel or personal problem. This may include health care professionals. Whatever the form of counselling for a teacher, it should be available to all staff, professional in its approach, impartial and confidential.

Once a manager is aware that a member of the teaching staff is suffering from stress, it may be prudent to find out if the stress is personal or work based. Or both. Giving support to a member of staff is paramount. It may take several discussions with reviews and action plans. Investing time as a manager may give improved results in the future.

If the stress is a personal problem, the manager may be able to provide support through giving their time to:

- listen to the problem;
- find alternatives and/or solutions;
- direct the teacher to a support service either in-house or through an external agency;
- provide information in the form of leaflets.

If the stress is workplace-based, the manager can:

- investigate the problem;
- develop strategies for assisting the teacher to cope;
- provide ongoing training and support.

Further ways for a manager to reduce stress

Job design

Good job design helps to clarify the roles of members of staff, thereby reducing role ambiguity and conflict. Additionally, utilizing all of a person's skills and, if appropriate, giving more responsibility may increase motivation and enthusiasm for the job.

Correct placement

By placing people in jobs that they are capable of doing, which are not beyond their ability, a manager can ensure that they are not over promoted or under utilized.

Career development

By planning careers and promoting people in accordance with their capabilities, avoiding over or under promoting.

Management training

To improve counselling skills and appraisal interview techniques, improve communication skills and other human-orientated skills that will assist in managing and reducing stress in others.

Motivation

Using methods of leadership and motivation that do not put excessive demands on staff.

'Walk in their shoes'

Many managers in education are former teachers and lecturers with little or no formal management training. In many cases, they have been appointed managers due to their long service or, sadly, by being in the right place at the right time. They may have only limited management training such as through in-house development schemes.

As was mentioned in Chapter 3, the culture of education has changed and the negative stressors are more intense, with the burden on the teacher increasing. Consequently, some educational managers may not be aware of current problems and/or do not possess the management skills necessary to solve problems. Although some managers may make suggestions for personal self-help, it may be that they themselves would benefit from similar advice, or even from returning to the 'root of the problem', by revisiting the classroom or lecture theatre. Once they have gained an insight into the current problems, they may be better placed to make improvements and suggestions.

Teacher burnout – and returning to work afterwards

Burnout can be described as a feeling of being helpless, disillusioned and depressed. It is often the result of untreated stress over a lengthy period of time where a teacher has desperately tried to cope on their own. The result is that usually the teacher is signed off work by their doctor.

It is often difficult for a teacher to return to work after such an absence. They might think that they have let the side down or feel unequal to their colleagues. To enable the teacher to return to work successfully, they have to be given support where appropriate. This may take the form of reduced hours in the first instance, a lighter workload or reduced administrative tasks.

Support given at this time is an investment for the teacher, the management of the school or college and the pupils. All three will benefit. More so, it is imperative that a school or college takes care of a person returning from absence due to stress. Failure to act with a duty of care may result in the teacher becoming ill again and the organization may be seen as negligent in its duty.

Conclusion

▋ Organizations need to understand how negative stress affects their staff.

I A stress checklist will identify major stressors.
I Education managers, not formally trained in management techniques, benefit from training.
I Organizations need to develop a strategy for reducing stress.
I Managers need to realize that stress exists.

Further reading

Also published by Kogan Page:

Armstrong, M (1998) _Managing People_
Dale, M (1998) _Developing Management Skills_, 2nd edn
Edenborough, R (1997) _Effective Interviewing_
Moon, P (1997) _Appraising Your Staff_, 2nd edn

6 *Reducing stress in teaching*

Chapter goals

This chapter aims to provide advice to those at operational level – the chalk face. It looks at:

- methods of delivery;
- assessment and grading;
- seeking support from others;
- moving forward.

A personal strategy for all in teaching

Making space and time for action

It has already been said that most stress in the work environment is caused by lack of time. Teachers are professionals and, in many cases, perfectionists. Why are they perfectionists? The answer lies in the fact that it is pointless passing on incorrect knowledge. Perfection, however, brings pitfalls which may lead to negative stress.

The following are some personal coping strategies, although the suggestions are not exhaustive. The impact of negative stress is a result of a personal variable and it must be remembered that what is right for you might not be always be successful for everyone. Similarly, different working or personal situations might require different techniques:

- timetable;
- innovative delivery;
- method of assessment;
- learning life skills;
- grading;
- peer group discovery;
- codes of conduct;
- parental involvement;
- social support;
- networking.
- being efficient *and* effective.

Timetable

If time is the first concern, then time needs to be prioritized and allocated. Students have timetables. A timetable tells them what they have to be doing at a certain time of the day. Teachers also have timetables which tell them what classes they have to teach at certain times of the day. How can we use our time more effectively?

Ask yourself these questions

- What hours do I teach?
- What hours do I need for preparation and marking?
- What time do I need for myself?
- What are my own personal commitments?

When you know the answers to the above, write *yourself* a timetable. Don't just include what you have to do for work. Include what you have to do for you. Allocate your time wisely. It may be that you like to work at home late in the evening. That's okay. Allocate it. You may like to get up really early each morning. That's okay. Allocate it. Stress, guilt and time are closely related. People get stressed because they don't have enough time for their family and friends. Allocate it.

Routine is important. It provides structure in which to work. A timetable is a routine, a framework. It is also a budget, a constraint. Where time is concerned, people get stressed because they feel guilty about what they should be doing instead of what they are doing. The answer may be this: allocate your time. Every hour. Once you have allocated it, stick to it. This will allow you to see clearly what time you have available. Time catches up on people because they overstretch themselves. Once you know what you have to do, including your own personal time, you can timetable in any requests from other people. It may be that you want to take on more. It may be that you don't have time for more. You can only create time by lessening time spent on something else. Therefore, when asked to take on more, see if it fits into your timetable.

Hint

You know what you need to do. Many teachers already have a timetable for their students, especially those needing motivation. Write one for yourself.

Innovative delivery

Consider the way that you teach. Is it chalk and talk, using a marker board, overhead projector, using technology, handouts, books and learning packs or other resource materials? Which methods produce the best results for your students? Which ones provide the inspiration for the students? Students generally want to learn and so, if the delivery interests them and they can relate to the subject matter, they will warm to it. They will become more self-disciplined, more interested, more enthusiastic and more demanding.

How can you integrate learning into the lives of the students? By relating it to what they know. A discussion on rules and regulations could integrate the rights and wrongs of a referee's recent and controversial decision in a football match. Foreign currency exercises could relate to a world tour of a pop group. Explore moral issues through soap operas. Every subject needs a motivation. Relate it to the students' understanding of the world and it will help them to see its relevance. Provide the inspiration and get away from the battle ground that so many teachers endure and relive through migraines, headaches, and all the other problems that stressed teachers suffer from.

Which delivery method gives you the best use of your time? You might feel that the best method for you is for the students to do a great deal of written work, copying from a board or screen. The question to ask yourself is this: if I used another method of teaching, would I have more time for myself?

Hint

Investigate alternative teaching methods. Use colleagues for discussion, support and networking.

Other methods may include role plays, case studies or in-tray exercises. Would I then be more refreshed and so be able to teach to a higher standard? What method would provide the best result for the learner?

Method of assessment

Assessing a student carries a range of options in much the same way as innovative delivery, although the choice may be restricted if the students are being prepared for an external formal examination. Internally set work, and the assessment of it, provide an opportunity for time, its creation and its management:

▮ Do the students have to write an essay?
▮ Do they have to complete an assignment?
▮ Do they have to make a presentation?
▮ Is it in the form of a video or tape?
▮ Do they have to make something? A model? A leaflet or booklet?
▮ Is it a case study?
▮ Are they working in pairs or groups?

Hint

Review the work you set. Are there any other methods that would enable the students to glean the same knowledge?

Learning life skills

Despite moving forward, education needs to further integrate itself into the working environment.This should be achieved through teaching and developing key skills and life skills, sometimes known as transferable skills. Much of the work of the future will be less paper-based and much more reliant on technology.

Using presentations for assessment

Presentations have two advantages. They provide time during an assessment for grading. They also provide a real situation. For example, suppose a section of the syllabus is on getting ready for work, conducting yourself at interviews, preparing questions and so on. A teacher could provide lessons on job descriptions, adverts, writing CVs, attending interviews, asking questions and general presentation skills. The teacher could assess all the written work that the student has done. The student could then read all their work before finally going off for a job interview. But by that time they may have forgotten much of what was taught. An alternative method of assessment could give a real live situation using role play, presentations, video and so on which will embed itself much more readily. The student will not only learn about interviews but will be able to use their memories and experience more easily than the written word. Experiential learning, learning through doing in a realistic environment, will support those in formal examinations too by enabling the student to recall situations enacted and then reinforced through a written or external exam.

How does this reduce stress in the teacher? Doesn't it create more because of the time it takes to organize the role play situation? It may do, but balance it out. Either assess each student individually using their portfolio/written work *or* assess a number of students at the same time. Decide which approach provides you with more time for action. Remember, another bonus of presentations is that they can't be taken home to grade, they have to be done there and then!

Hint

What methods of learning provide the students with systems used in a real work environment? What transferable skills do they learn?

Grading

Grading ties in with the assessment process yet it is different. In simple terms, assessment is the *method* used to judge a piece of work. Grading is the *value* given to a piece of work, and there are various methods of grading.

Grading is often subjective. Teachers deny this to their students, but most place students into categories from a very early stage. Consequently, a student will often fit into the grading range the teacher has pre-judged for them and their work. It is only when there are real changes from a student that the teacher notices and reviews the category that they are in. Subjective grading causes stress. Stress for the student, who has completed the work, and stress for the teacher, who may well be called upon by the student for an explanation as to why they were awarded a particular grade.

How can we reduce the subjectivity of grading? This is difficult. Taking it away from the teachers is not feasible, so what alternatives are there?

▪ Use technology for grading, by making use of computer-aided assessment for multiple choice tests, for example.
▪ Break the work down into small, easily graded, manageable parts so that a score can be given.

■ Assess using an ongoing method during assessment, ie presentations.

■ Grade according to a vocational industry requirement of competence. Have the students achieved the objective? Are they competent? Pass/fail?

■ Use peer groups. Tell the students to pass the work to the person sitting next to them and go through the work in class.

■ Go through the work in class and tell the students to make their own corrections.

There are many ways to grade work, and the important message to understand is that the teacher needs to use the most effective and efficient way for the task. If teachers collect in every piece of work from students, grade it themselves in a thorough and uniform manner, they will be doing a perfect job. . . as a grader. What they won't be doing is making time for action. There will be less time for teaching. The important aspect here is that a teacher gives feedback to students so that they can learn from past performance. Appraising a student's work may lead to their development through giving direction towards further reading.

It is important to realize that a teacher teaches and someone else or something else (technology) grades. The time spent grading could be better used in preparation or simply away from the task in hand to allow teachers to be more refreshed and ready for the next challenge.

Whatever method of assessment is chosen, it needs to be valid and reliable and enable the students to progress.

Hint

Match grading of work to the relevance and importance of the assessment.

Peer group discovery

Students gain almost as much learning and experiential learning from self discovery as they do from being taught by traditional methods. How does this reduce stress though?

Making the most of peer group discovery requires the teacher also to be a facilitator, helping the student by enabling them to find out where information is available. By doing this you become more effective and make more efficient use of your time, and the student gains the ability to discover up-to-date information and the knowledge to realize where and how they can update their own skills. Removing the stress of planning a lesson in favour of developing students' own learning skills from time to time will benefit teachers and students alike. Some things that are taught are obsolete almost as soon as the knowledge is passed on. The teacher may have spent a great deal of time preparing for the lesson only to find that within a short period of time the information is of no use. Providing research skills may be more advantageous for lifetime learning.

Hint

Ensure that *all* students participate in group work.

Codes of conduct

Often it is the cumulative occurrence of poor behaviour that can lead to negative stress and this may apply to both the student and the teacher. Discipline and self-discipline are key issues. Self-discipline is the conduct that is required of you in order to be professional in your job; discipline is seen as the punishment for bad behaviour. Discipline can also be pictured as the boundaries and parameters in which a person behaves; that is, what is acceptable and what is not. When a person behaves outside these parameters they become unacceptable and this is when a punishment is involved.

Discipline in schools and colleges is all about doing the right thing. Where there is acceptable behaviour, there is less negative stress – 'acceptable' being the key word. Codes of conduct have to be accepted by:

I the students;
I the teachers;
I the parents;
I the management.

Autocratic or democratic rules?

When should students be involved in the rule-making process? This depends on whether the need for a rule is on moral or common sense grounds. If it is about starting and finishing times for classes then it has to be imposed on the student and they should understand that it is not in their control. Schools with a uniform set dress codes at management level. Alternatively, if a rule is about smoking in the college common room, the students may issue their own rules which they can abide by.

Hint

Students should be involved in the development of a code of conduct. It is only through involvement and self responsibility that they will implement it.

Teachers are qualified to deal with discipline problems. They have the authority to do so and for this reason there has to be a policy that is accepted by the majority of staff and adhered to by *all* staff and students too, whether or not they *personally* agree with it.

Parental involvement

The key question here is: at what stage should parents cease to be involved in their child's education?

Teachers usually look forward to meeting the parents of the students they teach. They see education as a partnership where the teacher provides the knowledge and the specialism and the parent encourages the student to work hard and obey the ground rules. Parents, as discussed in Chapter 3, sometimes see the situation differently.

The argument for parental involvement is strong. At primary school level, parents become involved in committees and associations for fund-raising and similar activities. At senior/secondary school, they can attend parents' evenings, discuss optional subjects and help their child towards a career choice.

When students go on to post-16 education, many lecturers argue that the students are adults and that the parents need not be involved. At 18 the argument gets stronger. So where does the teacher or lecturer stop involving the parent? In truth, most parents would want to know if their child is causing concern – whatever their age.

There could be good cause to involve parents in the following situations, among others:

- Do they have a problem at home that the parent can help to solve?
- Are they on the wrong course?
- Have they been upset lately?

How can a school or college encourage parental support? There is a range of options including:

- parents' evenings;
- prizegivings;
- letters recognizing achievement;
- information on curriculum change;
- parent–governor relations;
- parent/teachers associations;
- letters advising of a problem;
- end of term reports.

A common problem is that a student does not always take information home for fear of his or her parents finding out that a problem exists. This is a hurdle that needs to be overcome, and solutions might include:

- letters without the college/school name either franked or printed on the envelope;
- hand-written envelopes;
- letters with a tear-off slip to be returned acknowledging receipt;
- reports that have to be acknowledged;
- homework books that have to be signed.

The above are just some suggestions. They are not suitable for every school or college and the list is practically endless.

Does positive parental involvement reduce negative stress? Yes, if the stress is a result of students' behaviour, lack of effort or ability or some other disciplinary problem, because having parental knowledge of a problem, and hopefully their support, goes a long way to sharing the problem and eventually solving it.

Hint

Developing a rapport with parents may help you to understand the needs, wants and motives of the student. It may also help when trying to enlist the support of parents.

Social Support

Lack of social support has been found to enhance levels of negative stress in teachers. Research has found that teachers with a family or a strong circle of friends are less susceptible to negative stress. Single teachers may lack social support at home and spend more time on their teaching. If the rewards of job satisfaction and student achievement are not forthcoming, they can become disillusioned and this may lead to stress. An ideal solution is to enjoy the company of a wide circle of friends, a particular partner, or both, and realize that there are opportunities for socializing outside the school environment. It is a fact of life that people generally like to be part of a group, a team to which they can respond.

Often social support is gained through a partner, relative or close friend who can play a valuable role listening, supporting, acknowledging and providing comfort. Friends and family can be a vital social support for anyone who is stressed. At times these relationships may become a life support when our own systems are malfunctioning.

Many people also find social support through group activities such as clubs, sports teams, hobbies and interests. These are all worth cultivating both in order to widen 'extra-curricular' activities and as a way of broadening social contact, which may eventually lead to social support.

Hint

Teaching is a job, not for life. Try alternative hobbies and interests and make time for the ones you enjoy.

Networking

Networking is the meeting of people in the same area of work. Many people suffering from negative stress feel that they are isolated. They look about in amazement at other people who appear to be coping with the same level and type of stressors. As discussed in earlier chapters, every individual has their own personality, their own *locus* of control which allows them to deal with problems in different ways. Networking often leads to the formation of support groups of like-minded people. Not necessarily support groups that people turn to when suffering from, for example, alcohol addiction, but more a group for sharing ideas or problems with. Talking about the negative stressors and problems can be cathartic. Some might say that this kind of support may lead to the individual being burdened with the problems of others, but this is not always the case. Sharing ideas with someone in a similar position may enable you to glean useful coping strategies and in turn pass on your own experiences and coping strategies for a problem they are dealing with. For example, if your personal stressor is a student who has a behavioural problem, one of your colleagues may have experience of the resources available to improve the situation. Meanwhile they may have a problem with a difficult manager, perhaps an experience you have previously dealt with successfully.

Hint

Tell colleagues about the difficulties you face. You are not alone. They will be able to help you.

Being efficient and effective

What is the difference between a teacher being efficient and a teacher being effective? Less negative stress. Being efficient may be described by traditionalists as doing the job as well as it was done in the past. Being effective is a skill that is less easy to measure in teaching. It is the passing on of knowledge in such a way that the students will comprehend answers and develop understanding and be able to apply it in future life, not necessarily as taught exactly, but maybe in some transferable way as the world of work develops.

Hint

Adopt strategies that make best use of your time and give the results you want.

Effectiveness is about getting effects. An effective teacher is one who is able to get the effects he or she wants. Effective, in a teaching context, is about being efficient to good purpose.

The teacher support network

The Teachers' Benevolent Fund (TBF) offers support to teachers, lecturers and their families regardless of age, length of service or union affiliation. *Teacherline*, the teacher support network, was launched in 1999 and is available twenty-four hours each day, every day of the year. It provides fully qualified counsellors who have all worked in or with the teaching profession and who understand the particular challenges facing teachers. This includes:

■ stress from workload, difficulties with colleagues, coping with OFSTED inspections;
■ relationship difficulties;
■ loss of confidence or motivation;
■ personal or family problems;
■ alcohol or drug dependency.

Providing a free, confidential service, they can be contacted in the UK on 0800 562 561 or at www.teacherline.org.uk.

Conclusion

Chapter 1 identified that teaching was a paradigm. Changes and developments in the way teachers teach, the behaviour of pupils and the administrative burden have been seen to be just some of the stressors teachers encounter everyday. Strategies have been suggested for the management, managers and teachers for lessening stress where it cannot be removed altogether. Yet stress reduction needs to be an ongoing process, one of discovery in an ever-changing world of education. The long-term solution is a partnership developed in three main areas.

1. *Excellence.* Schools, colleges and universities strive for this, although usually only in part. Excellence is made up of a whole range of elements. They include human resource strategy, industrial relations, Investors in People (IIP), improved results, higher qualifications.

2. *Innovation*. Innovation provides the edge, the opportunity to lead. New course development, new strategies, new teaching, new methods and new partnerships. Others may try to copy.

3. *Anticipation*. Anticipation provides the school, college or individual with the information to be in the right place at the right time. Trends in industry or vocational training. Trends in society. Students' aims and aspirations. Stress is a result of the changing culture in which we live. The ability to anticipate through divergent thinking increases the chances for success.

The pig and the sow

A story about the need to be open to change – innovative and developmental

Once, there was man who had a mountain retreat. At every opportunity he would drive there in his expensive car. He was very successful in business, thinking up new ideas, developing new projects and making money. The retreat was high up in the mountains and the man had to drive along a very dangerous road made up of blind curves, unguarded drops and difficult turns. The man was not bothered. He knew the road well, knew what the problems were and how to deal with them and he was a good driver. He had a good car with excellent road holding ability.

One day, as he was driving to the retreat, he approached a blind curve. He slowed down, braked slightly and changed gears in readiness for the bend. All of a sudden another car came around the curve, almost out of control. The second car nearly went off the edge of the mountain but at the last minute managed to get back onto the road, swerving from one side to the other.

The businessman thought that he was going to be hit, so he slowed down almost to a stop. The car came roaring on towards him, swerving back and forth. At the very last moment, it swerved back onto its own side of the road. As the two cars passed each other, a young woman stuck her head out of the car window and yelled as loud as she could, 'PIG!'

What? he thought, how dare she call me that! He was incensed by her aggressiveness, by her calling him a name. It was her fault after all. 'SOW!' he yelled after her, as she continued down the road.

I was in my own lane, he thought. How dare she call me that. As he regained control of his rage he felt more content. At least she hadn't got away with calling him names. He had given her what for and had exacted revenge, he thought to himself.

With that, he put his foot down, and drove around the bend straight into a pig.

This is a paradigm story. He thought that the woman was calling him a pig when in fact she was warning him. Despite the fact that she had nearly been killed, she took the time to warn him about the pig around the bend. The man had paradigm 'paralysis'. He thought that she had called him a pig and so he kept to the 'rules' and returned the compliment. He thought that would be the end of it.

If he had been more open, he would have said, 'What's happening?' In that case, he would have driven more slowly, would have seen the pig and dealt with it accordingly. At least he wouldn't have hit it!

The moral is this. In teaching, people have come from around blind corners. They may have argued, shouted, instructed and treated you badly. It may be that they haven't had time to stop and explain. The solutions come from within and it is up to you and your colleagues to work out the best solution for you given the paradigm, the set of rules, in which you are now working. If you have paradigm 'paralysis', you will only get negative stress. You will be frozen and not know what to do. If you are more open, you may see change as an opportunity and a challenge, a positive stressor.

Teaching is all about passing on knowledge – it is about providing someone with an education, the tools to equip them for life and its experiences. That will never change, but the methods will. Rules may change, but teaching staff have to be aware of the pig and the sow.

Further reading

Also published by Kogan Page:

Anderson, D, Brown, S and Race, P (1998) *500 Tips for Further and Continuing Education Lecturers*
Brown, S, Earplam, C and Race, P (1998) *500 Tips for Teachers*, 2nd edn
Race, P (1999) *2000 Tips for Lecturers*

7 *Other approaches to stress reduction*

Chapter goals

This chapter identifies a number of techniques for lowering the impact of stress. It looks at:

▌ identifying your own perception of a potential problem;
▌ taking control through a series of practical measures;
▌ suggesting a healthy lifestyle;
▌ introducing a range of supporting therapies.

Identifying the cause of stress

Chapter 2 showed that stress can be identified through a number of physiological or psychological symptoms in a similar way to many illnesses. For stress, as with any illness or disease, it is important to find the root cause of the problem and not just treat the symptom. The primary stage is to identify the cause of negative stress and not simply recognize and treat the reaction to it, the symptom. For example, continual headaches, skin rashes and insomnia can be treated with pain killers, creams and sleeping pills. However, the underlying cause would remain, and, long term, it is this that needs to be treated rather than the symptom.

Adapting to stress can bring about changes which may prove helpful. These may include changing jobs, moving house or changing relationships. Alternatively, the only solution may be to come to terms with the problem and accept the realities of the situation. Acceptance often reduces stress in itself. A useful mental exercise is to remember how you dealt with a problem in the past. However, the strategies previously used may no longer be of value as the workload may have changed, or the use of new technology may have introduced a different method of working.

Hint

Don't just ignore stress. Identify the cause and take action to remove it or at least lessen the effect.

Holistic solutions

Taking a global or holistic outlook, stress reduction opportunities can include:

- changing yourself;
- changing your relationships;
- changing your activities;
- changing your attitudes.

Each of these changes interacts; for example, changing your attitude may affect your relationships. It is not possible to simply take only one of the above as a solution when a combination of all four strategies may be the answer. There is no simple cure-all for stress and yet the removal of even a minor problem may leave an individual in a better position to cope.

Remember, learning to cope with stress needs to be a gradual process rather than a one-off enthusiasm, an obsession or a millennium resolution to be dealt with by 1 January. Like the crash diet that actually adds more weight in the long term, a 'crash' stress policy may similarly cause extra stress. So approaches to stress reduction need to be considered, planned, realistic and ongoing.

The effects of personality

An individual's personality affects their perception and reaction to external stresses. It can even be a source of stress in its own right and may also influence a person's way of coping.

Personality traits affect people's choice of confidant, their explanation and reasoning behind problems and their receptiveness to suggestions for improvement. The complexity of a problem can be compounded by certain personality characteristics such as being withdrawn, paranoid, passive, neurotic, obsessional, introspective, aggressive or anxious. In order to tackle stress it is important to try and understand how your personality affects your response to stress.

Dealing with stress may also result in the denial or distorting of reality. These so called 'defence' mechanisms include the following.

Rationalization. A means of self-deception where the person suffering from stress finds satisfactory and socially acceptable reasons for behaviour. For example, failure to get a new job or even an interview for a new job may be rationalized, and therefore minimize stress, by asserting that the promotion would not have been as advantageous as first thought. Many years ago there was an advert on television for a chocolate bar in which a young woman was stood-up on a date. On returning home, and eating the chocolate, she then said of her date, 'He had buck teeth anyway,' therefore rationalizing that she was better off without him.

Projection. The blame is attributed to something or someone else, as in a bad workman blaming his tools. Professionals may blame their equipment, the computer that crashes, for example, or colleagues who don't behave in a professional way. Teachers may also attribute poor performance and results to the lack of skills of their students. It may be that they are in a deprived area, it may be that they have learning difficulties, it may be that they have other distractors. It may be that the teacher is having difficulty coping.

Diversionary tactics. The diversion or displacement of emotional emphasis from one object to another. For example, a new hobby. It may also take the form of attacking one object when one cannot attack the real stressor, such as banging a table instead of a person.

Withdrawal. Becoming withdrawn from a situation, daydreaming and being apathetic. Lack of focus is often a prime indicator of someone suffering from negative stress. Continual daydreaming, discussing side issues or non-involvement are often the result of a non-coping situation. Teachers unable to cope are often seen to be disinterested. Students as a result might become noisy, disruptive and aggressive, which in turn adds to the stress facing the teacher.

Infancy or regression. Returning to dependency when decisions are made by others and when the opportunity or requirement to make decisions may be passed to others. Consequently, while group work is seen as a useful tool for developing new techniques or for brainstorming, it often hides those who are coping with the workload and those who are suffering.

Denial. Persuading yourself that the stressors have not happened, in the hope that they will go away.

Taking control

> Grant me the serenity to accept the things I cannot change, the courage to change the things I cannot accept and the wisdom to know the difference.

One way to lessen the effects of negative stress is to take control of the stressors before their negativity takes control. In other words, an individual needs to take ownership and control of stressful situations by breaking out of the victim role and developing an owner mentality. The precursor for this is to place stressful events into four categories:

▌ important and controllable;
▌ important and uncontrollable;
▌ unimportant and controllable;
▌ unimportant and uncontrollable.

Once the event has been placed into one of the above categories, the individual may be better placed to realize the skills necessary to resolve the problem and to use them for self benefit. These may be awareness skills, acceptance skills, coping skills or action skills. Practical examples of the above four categories are as follows:

Important and controllable

If you don't like the school that you teach in, you first need to be aware of the options available to you. What part of the school don't you like? Is it the building itself, the available resources, the rules and regulations? Once you identify the problem and have identified what would be more suitable for you, then you may be in a better position to do something about it. This may include changing schools, moving to a new area, or leaving the profession.

Important and uncontrollable

An example may be that you don't like the administrative or testing system in primary schools. You need to accept this, as it is beyond your control. The coping strategy here is to identify what aspect you don't like. Is it the actual tests or the way in which they are administered? It may help to discuss it with colleagues to seek out how they feel about it, or use colleagues as an information source for new ideas.

Unimportant and controllable

If you spend all your free time marking students' work and have little time for yourself or your family, you may need to look at your own work methods. Possible solutions to this problem were dealt with in Chapter 6, but you may have to accept that at certain times of the year the workload is very high. The answer is to select the best possible solution even if it does not totally resolve the problem.

Unimportant and uncontrollable

There are two things to consider here. Firstly, it is not always possible to control some events although it may be possible to control reactions to the problem. Secondly, of what level of importance is an event to you? If a colleague you feel is less qualified than you gets a promotion at another school, there is not much that you can do about it. Acceptance may be the answer. At this point you must decide how you want your career to progress. Do you want added responsibility or extra travelling time? Is a promotion of value to you? If you decide you want a similar promotion you will have to acquire a set of skills and qualifications to make you more suitable than other candidates and actively seek out opportunities.

The four categories above, together with the examples given, use the skills of action, coping, accepting and awareness. The final skill is that of desire, positively wanting to be less stressed, and thus stopping yourself from carrying the stress with you.

Personal factors that seem to play an important part in determining resistance to negative stress are those of optimism, pessimism and hardiness. Optimists are much less likely to report physical illness and symptoms than pessimists during highly stressful situations. Hardy people, it is suggested, differ in that they have higher levels of commitment, self control and personal belief, and the perception that challenges are opportunities.

Four broad complementary strategies to lessen the impact of negative stress

The following strategies may be useful in dealing with negative stress:

∎ training the attention, clearly focusing on a particular problem;
∎ increasing control over thought processes with systematic and logical reasoning;
∎ increasing the ability to handle emotions by deciding whether or not a problem is within your control;
∎ aiding physical relaxation for issues that may be outside your control.

These broad strategies work in partnership with the alternative approaches below, but cannot be grouped as above because they overlap between two or more. Alternative approaches include:

∎ deep muscle relaxation;
∎ meditation;
∎ hypnotherapy and self hypnosis;
∎ exercise, such as yoga, sport and hobbies;

■ religion;
■ Alexander technique;
■ acupuncture;
■ reflexology;
■ homeopathy;
■ herbal medicine;
■ aromatherapy;
■ macrobiotic diets;
■ Shiatsu massage.

In addition to those listed above, many people seek to lessen the effects of stress through alcohol or drugs – prescribed or otherwise. These ultimately mask the causes of stress and only alleviate the symptom in the short term. They also risk dependency if they are used or misused as a way of tackling stress or indeed any other problem.

Improving your health in general can help lessen the effects of stress on the body. When the body is run down, minor problems can multiply. Commonsense measures for stress reduction, therefore, should always include:

■ a sensible diet;
■ getting the right amount of sleep that you need;
■ taking regular exercise;
■ cutting down on alcohol and caffeine intake where possible.

Practical measures

Creating time for action

Many of the negative stressors people suffer from are caused by lack of time. Our time is in demand. It is a valuable resource and there is rarely enough of it. Improving your management of time could well help to significantly reduce any stress that you may be experiencing.

We may feel stressed because we don't have time to do something in the way that we want. Or we haven't got time for ourselves. So how can we extend the time available to us? By making better use of it – and there are several ways you might do this:

Making lists

Most people write lists for shopping or a list of the things that they have to do. Lists are useful tools not just to aid your memory but also as a way of being cathartic. It is a way of writing down all the negativity in your life and, by doing so, seeing them in a different light and to some extent releasing the ill effects that they cause. A list can help reduce negative stress in one of two ways. Firstly, it acts as a reminder of what a person needs to do. People often get stressed because they have forgotten to do something, so by using a list the problem can be solved. A list of what has to be done creates time because it acts as an instant reminder, so avoiding wasting time trying to remember tasks in hand. Secondly, although not directly connected to time, it is a good idea to write down all the stressors in your life, both positive and negative, in two separate columns. (Remember that positive stress is useful, it provides us with a challenge or opportunity.) These two columns can be concerned with relationships, aspects of work, financial constraints and responsibilities, business, partners and so on. Once these stressors have been written down, it is easier to visualize them and to focus on the impact that they have on your life.

The next stage is to review each negative stressor and try to formulate a plan to either remove it from the list or to see it in a different light, maybe as an opportunity. It is this stage that makes personal space and time.

For example, if your family is demanding too much of your time, that is, acting as a chauffeur for Brownies on a Monday, swimming on a Tuesday, piano on a Wednesday and so on, you could try to make time for yourself by working as a team with other parents and sharing the load. You will soon discover that you are not alone and that other families have exactly the same stressors. If you have too many financial ties, explore ways to remove or alter them. Do you have any luxuries that are unnecessary? Does your child need a mobile phone? Will a pager system suffice? Can you prepare food in bulk on one day each week to save you cooking every day? Can your family support you in any other way – cooking, cleaning, running errands and so on?

Hint

Writing down the stressors may help you visualize them and in doing so make you identify the skills necessary to remove them.

Stop being a hero

In conjunction with the list as above, it is time to look at aspects of your day-to-day life that are of value and make choices. Everyone has needs and wants, but it is impossible to do everything. Consequently, some of the stressors people are faced with are self inflicted and could be removed. Look closely at what is important to you. Career? Home? Family? Relationships? By removing the negativity of the stressors that are not important, you gain more energy to deal with the negative stressors that *are* important. You cannot remove *all* the negative issues in your life, but by removing the unimportant ones you create time for the rest.

Delegation

Delegation is another useful tool that can be used both at home and at work. It is not always easy to get someone to do something that you have always done yourself. They might feel resentful, but conversely they might not have wanted to get involved before because they thought that the particular task was one that you enjoyed. Letting go may also prove difficult, and one of the hard facts about delegation is the realization that someone else's way might be different from your own. Remember that just because it is different doesn't mean that it is wrong. As long as the end result is satisfactory then you have removed one of the negative issues in your life. Sharing a load takes away some of the pressure – remember the old saying: 'a problem shared is a problem halved'.

> ## Hint
>
> Delegate tasks and responsibilities at home and at work. Remember that people have different approaches to tasks and that doesn't always mean they are wrong.

Say 'No'

Have you ever said *'No'*? When you are asked to do something, take the time to think about what is being asked of you. Consider this before you decide:

- Is it important?
- Is it necessary?
- Are you the only one that can do it?
- Is it something that you want to do?
- Is there something else that you should be doing?

> ## Hint
>
> 'Sorry, I'm busy. I don't have the time. I can't manage that. . .'

Assertive or aggressive?

Many people confuse being assertive with being aggressive. They often see someone who stands up for their rights, someone who demands fairness and equality, as being aggressive. Being assertive means affirming or being positive in your approach. Aggressive means to attack and be on the offensive, often in an unprovoked incident.

This issue ties in with learning to say *'no'*. It is important to consider what is reasonable and what is not, what is acceptable to you and what is not. Unassertive people frequently do not express irritation over the little things in life. They carry around a whole range of tormentors, appearing cool on the outside, until one day they blow up totally unexpectedly, over the slightest problem.

It is important to learn to communicate unhappiness, displeasure and frustration in a way that is acceptable socially. Assertive people speak from their own point of view, take responsibility for their feelings and try to help others understand why they are upset. On the other hand, aggressive people will say what they think, often in an abusive manner.

Aggressiveness and assertiveness can be compared as shown in Table 7.1.

Table 7.1 Aggressive or assertive?

Aggressiveness	Assertiveness
Leads to feelings of embarrassment and guilt	Seldom followed by embarrassment and guilt
Often makes enemies and aggravates situations	Allows others to comprehend your point of view
Usually results in a negative outcome	Is more likely to achieve a positive outcome

---

Hint

Learn to be firm, not angry.

A healthy lifestyle

Food

When people feel the impact of negative stress they often have one of two reactions and either stop eating properly or they binge on all the wrong foods. The former is a result of loss of appetite or a feeling of nausea. In many cases there may be some weight loss; if you lose weight dramatically without trying it is important that you see your doctor as soon as possible. Bingeing is often seen as a comfort, a release, a way of enjoyment. Often it is also a way of distracting your thoughts away from the stress.

The following are basic eating guidelines. Don't try them all at once as this will increase your level of stress. Remember that the intention is to reduce the stress, so they are only guidelines and what may be right for you may not be right for someone else.

Drink plenty of fluids, especially water and fruit juice. Avoid fizzy drinks if possible, as they tend to cause bloating. One of the best things that you can avoid in order to improve your handling of stress is caffeine drinks. These not only include coffee, but also tea, some colas and some 'soft' drinks now available that are designed to give you a quick lift. Caffeine is a drug, a stimulant for the central nervous system. It may make you feel more alert temporarily but in the long term can make you feel jittery and, in some cases, depressed. Being a drug, it may also be habitual in some people and by not drinking coffee or cola you may find that you suffer from headaches in the short term until the caffeine in your body has gone.

Hint

Eat small portions of food that you particularly like. They are your treats and you can use them as incentives in order to get jobs done when negative stress has made you feel lethargic.

Do not rush your meals. Take time to eat properly. Don't just grab a sandwich while on the run from one place to another. Time spent eating is a good way to refresh yourself not just with food but also a good time to think and reflect, refreshing the brain and giving a new found enthusiasm.

Eat balanced meals with a selection of proteins, carbohydrates, minerals and vitamins. Try to eat less fat and fatty food, especially those containing saturated fats and cholesterol. Increase dietary fibre intake by eating more fresh fruit and vegetables, whole grain cereals and pulses and try to eat less sugar and salt. Avoid junk food. Most people eat junk food or fast food because of the convenience and time-saving factor. It's ready prepared and cooked and all you have to do is eat it. But it often contains all the wrong ingredients for a healthy diet. However, don't feel guilty about what you eat.

Hint

Decide what is right for you, what you feel comfortable with, and most of all try to enjoy your time spent eating.

Taking breaks

A break from an activity is an ideal way of seeing it in a new light. You will often find that if you leave a task for a while, when you go back to it you will see a new opportunity or angle for investigation. The time spent having a break is well spent. The more time we spend on something without taking a break, the less efficient we become and the more mistakes we make.

Hint

Don't work every evening or weekend. Plan to take a break, and take time for yourself.

Some people at work don't give themselves time for a morning break or a lunch break because they feel that they are just too busy. In this case they need to *create* time for themselves because making space may increase creativity, while not taking time may lead to lethargy, mistakes and creative block.

Learning to relax

Relaxation is something that most people don't do enough of. It is the time when you are at rest mentally and physically. Many times people *say* they are relaxing because they are sitting down doing nothing demanding, such as watching the television, and yet their minds may still be working, thinking of what else they have to do.

One way to relax is to do some relaxation exercises. These have the effect of slowing your heart rate and so making you feel more at ease. Some simple relaxation/breathing exercises can be done anywhere, not just when you are in a quiet room. They may help when you are on your way home on the train or bus or stuck in a traffic jam, or when waiting at the checkout in the supermarket. A simple breathing exercise may release tension and put you in a better state of mind.

Hint

Sit in a comfortable chair or lie down in a warm room.
Make sure you are not interrupted.
Relax your arms and legs by uncrossing them.
Take your shoes off.
Lean into the chair or lie back on the sofa or bed.
Close your eyes and be aware of your body.
Breathe in slowly through your nose and out through your mouth.
Breathe deeply.
Visualize something you enjoy, such as a picture, a family member or partner, or a hobby.

Other relaxation exercises take longer. They may include the use of specific floor exercises while listening to a tape telling you how to relax each part of your body. Tapes are available for a wide range of subjects, including stress reduction, diet, smoking and low self-esteem.

Sleep

How much sleep do we need? Some people can't manage on less than nine hours each night. Others can manage on four or five. Some people manage on a few hours sleep providing that they catnap during the day. The Spanish siesta is ideal for some, although others would argue that if they sleep during the day they wouldn't be able to sleep at night. Can we catch up on sleep? If we only have two hours sleep one night do we need twelve hours the next to make up sleep time?

There are no fixed rules about how much sleep an individual needs. However, there are fixed rules about the quality of sleep that we get. Many people who can't sleep at night or wake during the night soon start to worry about it. This is normal, but worrying compounds the problem and the worry then affects their sleeping. It is this worrying about not being able to sleep that causes more of a problem than the actual loss of sleep. The answer may lie in one of the following:

- Don't eat too late at night.
- Avoid drinks that have stimulants in them in the evening. These include coffee, tea, cola.
- Have a warm drink
- Do something relaxing last thing at night. Don't start on a new project that will make your mind more alert.
- Enjoy a warm bath or shower.
- Don't work until the last possible moment and then expect to be able to get straight to sleep. Relax first.
- Get into a routine. Try to sleep at the same time every day.
- If you can't get to sleep, get up. Do something positive rather than look at the clock and worry about what time you will get to sleep. You could read a book. Do the ironing. Listen to some relaxing music.
- If you are mulling over a problem and can't sleep because your mind is too alert, write down all your ideas. Make a list of things that you have to do. You can then reassure yourself that there is nothing more to do and you may find it easier to get to sleep.

▌ If you wake up very early and can't get back to sleep, then get up and do something positive. You may feel more energetic as a result and therefore likely to sleep better the following night.

Socializing/recreation time

Having time for socializing and recreation is important. It combines the theory of creating space and time for action and taking time out for yourself. It should always be something that you enjoy and could be simply going to the pub with friends, eating out, or embarking on a new hobby. The type of recreational activity is not important as long as you enjoy it, as this in itself reduces stress.

Like all activities taken up as a hobby, they only work as stress busters when they are enjoyable. The minute they become a chore they are failing in their objective. For example, if you take up tennis but find that the nearest tennis club is five miles away and that to get there you have to sit in traffic jams, it may then become a stressor and not a stress buster. It may be time to move on and find an alternative.

Alcohol

Alcohol in moderation can be a stress buster. Many people enjoy a drink after work as it provides the perfect opportunity to unwind and relax. It may be a social event. It may make you think differently and see a problem in a new light.

The problem arises when alcohol intake becomes excessive. In this case alcohol will hide the problem, masking the cause and only alleviating the symptom. Generally recommended drinking levels are 14 units of alcohol spread across each week for women, 21 for men, with one unit roughly equalling one glass of wine, although this depends on an individual's alcohol tolerance level. Although a weekly limit is suggested, it should be noted that it is not wise to save up the units each day and then have 14 units on a Friday or Saturday night. This may reduce stress in the short term, but the hangover may be worse and it is not a healthy solution. Excessive or prolonged alcohol consumption may lead to high blood pressure, cirrhosis of the liver and heart disease.

Hint

Everything in moderation.

Holidays

Some people don't take all their holiday entitlement because they believe they are far too busy or that they are indispensable. Employers give holiday time because they know that the time will allow employees to recharge their batteries and refresh themselves. When they return they are more likely to have higher levels of energy and enthusiasm for the job in hand and may bring about some new ideas.

A holiday is only such if it takes you away from your normal routine. In many cases, taking a week off work and continuing the same routines as normal fails to provide the right form of break. A holiday needs to provide a change of scenery, a different routine where you cannot solve work-based problems and are not just a phone call away should they need you.

Sometimes an individual feels that they need a holiday but doesn't have much of their entitlement left. A solution might be to take a day or two off and stay at home. This is not ideal, as odd days away from the workplace while still at home may not provide an adequate break. A solution might be to take a long weekend and leave your normal environment. It is this change of scenery and location that acts as the stress buster in many cases.

Holiday entitlement for teachers has changed in many areas of education. Historically, teachers were only allowed holiday time during school holiday periods, but were then entitled to leave for the complete length of the break. Changing contracts in some colleges and universities, especially those teaching all year round, now means some teachers have a set holiday entitlement, which differs from the number of days the college or university is closed to students. As a result, some leave may be allowed during term time. A long weekend break is idyllic during a long and hard term!

Hint

Take time away, not just time off. Enjoy a change of routine.

Exercising

Exercise is useful in that it helps to keep the body trim and fit. We all need some form of exercise, ideally on a regular basis. Exercise also helps by:

- using up excess energy that may cause insomnia;
- providing a pleasurable experience;
- occupying the mind away from negative stress;
- being a social activity.

There are many forms of exercise and for most people the easiest one is walking. Walking for 20 minutes each day exercises the body and mind. It helps the body because it reduces tension by lowering the levels of adrenaline. The bonus is the effect that walking has on the mind. It provides an opportunity to get away from the stressful situation and in many cases provides the time to think more clearly and creatively. Most people would say that they don't have time to walk, that they need to use the car. This argument goes back again to the strategy of creating time and space for action, giving yourself the opportunity to take exercise. Even a short walk helps.

There is a whole range of other exercises and activities that are useful for health and well-being. Many are at different levels of skill so that we don't need to be an expert to take part. Some are contact sports and some are more gentle. Each has its own attributes and the best one is the one that you are able to do, feel comfortable with, have time to do and enjoy.

While sport and exercise can be a stress buster, you need to think carefully about how involved you want to become. For example, if you take up a sport for the enjoyment, you may not want the additional pressure of competition. Similarly, for some sports you may need a partner or opponent and that person may not always be available. However, the advantage of sport and exercise is that they can bring about a positive stress or new challenge.

Hint

Enjoy the exercise but don't become too obsessed with it – or let it become another stressor.

Complementary therapies

These are supporting therapies that won't remove the source of the stress but may lessen its negative impact.

- *Meditation.* This consists of a range of techniques for contemplation and concentration. They can be effective in controlling blood pressure and migraines. Most meditators spend 15/20 minutes twice a day in a quiet, comfortable place.
- *Yoga.* This is for physical and mental relaxation. It consists of exercises in posture to condition the body and clear the mind. The aim is to have the ability to hold the positions for an extended period of time without movement or distraction, or to run through a sequence of positions.
- *Aromatherapy.* This is the use of pure essential oils in order to soothe tension and improve health and well-being. The oils can be massaged into the body, used in the bath or inhaled.
- *Acupuncture.* This ancient Chinese medical treatment is used to relieve pain, cure illness and improve general health. It can also be used to support a person's motivation to give up smoking, or to diet more effectively or solve any other habitual problem.

It consists of inserting a number of needles, called 'meridians', into various parts of the body. It is a treatment that aims to alter the flow of a person's bodily energy or life force to relieve pain and restore health.

- *Autogenics*. This method of self-hypnosis, developed in the 1930s, emphasizes individual control over body processes through specific exercises. Training takes between two and three months, with standard exercises aimed at inducing a feeling of well-being and a coping ability. Specific exercises deal with breathing, blood flow and skin temperature – all associated with the effects of negative stress.
- *Alexander Technique*. This is viewed as more of a way of life rather than a therapy in that it teaches people new ways of using their bodies with a view to eliminating bad habits that people are not aware of, such as poor posture. The technique improves both physical and psychological well-being.

Acceptance

If the symptoms of negative stress get too much to bear, don't be afraid to talk to your doctor. In the short term, medication may be able to help. It is perfectly normal for people to feel stressed at times due to their workload. If the problem can be discussed, it can more often that not be solved. Your doctor will be able to recommend a counsellor for you to talk to, someone outside your normal circle of friends and colleagues, who will be able to take a clear view of your stress and support and guide you to find solutions.

Hint

Don't be put off going to the doctor by feelings of low self-esteem, inadequacy or the myth that stress is only for the weak. It isn't, and by solving the problem you are helping your employer.

Key issues

▌ Stress reduction opportunities are based on an individual's ability to cope.

▌ Realization of a problem is the first step in any stress reduction technique.

▌ Techniques and opportunities for stress reduction may take a physical or mental strategy.

▌ Strategies are individual and will have advantages and disadvantages which may or may not be suitable for each person.

▌ Stress reduction techniques must be dealt with rationally in order not to generate further negative stress through panic and desperation.

Conclusion

Drawing on the theories and points discussed, you should consider all of the following points when planning and managing your stress:

▌ It is important at all times to keep a positive self-image and not engage in negative self-fulfilling prophecies.

▌ You should learn to be assertive.

▌ Make time and use it wisely for forward planning to anticipate, innovate and excel.

▌ Whenever you attempt a new method to cope with stress, identify the successful and unsuccessful elements of the strategy.

▌ Recognize the true and relevant sources of stress and not simply the often wrongly assumed source.

▌ Identify a stress reduction technique that has previously worked.

▌ Widen your social circle in order to network and reduce stressors through social support.

▌ Try where possible to bring feelings out into the open.

▌ Try to say 'No' to unnecessary demands.

▌ Try to come to terms with each individual situation.

▌ Get your priorities right about what is important to you.

▌ Enjoy yourself with your friends and family.

▌ Learn to delegate.

■ Make small but regular changes to your lifestyle but do not embark on a crash 'stress' diet.

■ Seek the support of your doctor if you are worried about your health.

■ Get to know yourself better. Find out what is right for you.

■ Treat yourself when appropriate.

■ Think realistically about what is achievable and what is not.

■ Get involved in activities where the negative stressors are partially or fully removed from your mind for a while, such as sport, hobbies, meditation, or relaxation techniques.

■ Try where possible to improve your lifestyle, diet and sleeping habits.

■ Make space and create time for action.

And finally . . .

The ten commandments for reducing negative stress:

1. Thou shalt not be perfect or even try to be.
2. Thou shalt not try to be ALL things to ALL people.
3. Thou shalt leave things undone that ought to be done.
4. Thou shalt not spread thyself too thinly.
5. Thou shalt learn to say 'No'.
6. Thou shalt schedule time for thyself and support network.
7. Thou shalt switch off and do nothing – regularly.
8. Thou shalt be boring, inelegant, untidy and unattractive at times.
9. Thou shalt not feel guilty.
10. Thou shalt not be thine own worst enemy but be thine own best friend.

Appendix 1: Case studies

All the case studies are true. Sadly, many managers still don't recognize that stress exists, or that if it does, consider it to be the 'fault' of the stressed person. For this reason, to protect the individual, some of the personal details have been excluded.

Primary school teacher

Cathy teaches at an independent girls' school.

'This is my fourth term in this school, although I have been teaching for about 13 years. The girls range in age from 3–11. I teach the reception class so all the pupils are four or five. Because it is an independent school, we don't have tests at 7 or 11 although most of the 11-year-olds have tests for senior school entry. We don't have to publish any of the school results.

'My stress comes from the fact that I set high standards for myself. I have high expectations. Many teachers are perfectionists. The group size can be a problem. There are 27 pupils of mixed ability. I do get support from a classroom assistant, which is really good, but if she is sick, she isn't replaced. If another teacher is sick, she often has to cover them. I have to listen to all the pupils read and that's where the help is great. Without her, it is really difficult. She's also there if one of the girls has an "accident". They are only four or five years old.

'I don't take a proper lunch break although I do take a morning break. Listening to all these children read wouldn't be possible otherwise. We don't have any behaviour problems at this school, unlike my last school. That is a state school in a London borough. I now get excellent support from a good headteacher. She is willing to meet parents and staff and has an open door policy, which I think is really good. Generally, parents are very supportive of the work we do but some have high expectations and are a bit critical.

'During term time, I have no social life. Every night I do some preparation for the next day. For the class I teach there's not much marking, although some of my colleagues, who teach older pupils, mark for two hours each night. I am too tired for preparation on a Friday night and so sometimes I have to do it at the weekends. I have three children of my own and so the weekend is also taken up with shopping, cleaning and ironing.

'The pay is about the same as at a state school. I thought that the holidays might be more, but in fact I only get one day more than my daughter. I have great support from my husband and am lucky to have a good childminder. If she is sick, though, I may have to call on my father to be the stand-in minder. I have been known to drive over to collect him at six in the morning. Teaching and running a family requires you to be really well organized.

'Before the first OFSTED inspection at my last school, it was a school in crisis. Out of 16 teachers, 12 left. The headteacher took early retirement and the replacement was awful. That shows that the support of the headteacher really works. The worst time in many schools is before an OFSTED inspection. My doctor says that is her busiest time for seeing teachers. Before OFSTED and the National Curriculum there was no paperwork. I think the National Curriculum is a good idea but it has been chopped and changed too much. I don't think there was much consultation, especially with people involved with children.

'Whatever I have said, I do love my job. It's very rewarding. I do think that we should have a compulsory break every five years. We would come back refreshed. In Ireland, where my brother teaches, their job is held open. We need long holidays to recover. Without them, it gets very tiring. I am in support of job sharing and I think this would help a lot of people. Teaching is a rewarding career but there is more to life than teaching and it's just a case of getting your priorities right and learning to live.'

UK inner city headteacher

Miss H is the headteacher at a primary school in the north west of England.

'My first day here was awful. The school was small but dreadful and I was a very new teacher. It was something I found difficult to imagine. My teaching practices had been nothing like this. There were 67 pupils on the school roll but on most days only about 40 would turn up. The building was run down, the pupils often played truant and staff turnover was faster than McDonald's. School inspectors almost closed the school because they thought it was a danger to the children. About a month after I started, the then headteacher left because she was stressed and couldn't cope any more. I was the only full-time teacher left at the school and my first thought was to pack up and leave. I used to look in the mirror every morning and think to myself, "What have I done?" The stress was enormous and I would suffer from stomach cramps as a result. Every day on my way home, if I saw some children from the school, I used to walk the other way. I couldn't take any more.

'But I hung on. I was pretty stubborn and I saw something in the children. Yes, they were rowdy, but they didn't know how to behave, what to do. That's why the school was failing. That's why they rebelled. They had been let down and were disillusioned. Many times they were sent home because there were no teachers to teach them. On the other days they couldn't be bothered. The system was failing them. The school had such a bad name that even supply teachers didn't want to come here. In one term we had about two supply teachers each week. The reception class had one teacher, it still has, only one, Miss Jones. All the other classes had two for safety. The building was in a terrible state. Rain came in, ceilings collapsed, mould grew inside. The only running water was in the boys' toilets.

'When the old headteacher gave up, I was left with only the school secretary for support. She is still here, and she is great. I couldn't have lasted without her support and her words of comfort when things got tough. The first thing we did was paint the classrooms. They were left over from the nineteenth century and needed brightening up. Once the pupils started coming back we began to focus on discipline. They needed to know what we would tolerate and what we wouldn't. We made the rules together and every year the pupils revised them. They do get out of date, times change. The children put up a poem they had written in the corridor. It's all about having respect for people, not telling lies and doing the best you can. The first time I read it I cried.

'At first, I used to ring the bell in the playground and the children would ignore it and carry on playing. I started giving prizes for the best lines, the best students. I wanted the children to try, to do their best, and see the rewards. They needed an incentive. It's not really any different now, except I don't reward with biscuits, I reward with praise for good work and that stimulates them to try harder.

'The school is near a very run-down estate where there is crime, drug dealing and hardship. The local authority was undecided about the school's future and had considered pulling it down and starting again. The majority of children come from families on benefit, where English is the second language and not spoken at home. The children did an exercise recently on languages throughout the world. Children at our school speak over 20 different languages and dialects.

'The parents are now much more involved. They can see results. Many help out on committees and they are always trying to raise money for us for new equipment, new facilities and materials. They don't have much in the way of money to offer, but they offer their time and they have some great ideas of what will and what won't work. The last fundraiser was a disco on a Saturday afternoon which raised over £150, with raffles and prizes for the best dancers. Some parents even come in to supervise at playtime and dinner time.

'We try to make learning interesting. It has to provide an inspiration for the children. And the children need to see when they have done well, and when they need more help. Rewards come in different shapes to the old days. I don't often have to look for new teachers any more, they like to stay here, but when I am looking I go and see every applicant at their current school. I want to see how they deal with the children, how they cope, how they teach, what methods they use and how they inspire them to aim high. I soon learnt that some teachers are just good at interviews and not very good at teaching. I needed to find the right sort of people. When I first came here, the children didn't leave the building for fear of what they might do. Now we go on visits to all sorts of places and we are even planning a week away. We have a choir and do concerts and plays and the hall is always full of parents. They help out with scenery and costumes. I owe a great deal to the parents who supported me from the early days here. It was through them that other parents brought their children here. They gave me that chance to prove that it could work.

'The school has grown too and we have a waiting list. When I first came here, children had a reading age of 6 when they were 10. Now they all have above average results. At the last inspection, the OFSTED inspector reported that we were a very good school. We had an excellent report for planning, assessment, leadership and management. I still get stressed but not for the same reasons. Now we have been recognized as a good school we just have to keep it up. That's what the children deserve. They deserve the chance, they deserve the best. They are tomorrow.'

Secondary school (from age 11 to 16/18)

'After I qualified, my first teaching job was at a large comprehensive school next to a notorious council estate. Stress levels for all the staff at the school are immensely high, mainly due to pupil behaviour. Teaching is not the word to describe what I did at the school, but rather riot control. It was a struggle to get highly unmotivated, disinterested teenagers to sit and listen, let alone to put pen to paper. Classes were taught in mixed ability sets, which meant absolute chaos in lower set groups, even though the class sizes were around 25. The whole day was stressful, as lunch times generally consisted of supervising meaningless detentions.

'Although I have painted a bleak picture of this school, it did have its high points. The smoking room was the place to be at break times as teachers would talk incessantly to one another while puffing out smoke and relating the horrors of 8P4 that morning. Different methods of dealing with various pupils floated through the air, along with terrible jokes, just to keep our spirits up. Individually, the pupils were great, but it was impossible for them to leave their troubled lives at home. The only way to get rid of stress was to talk. It soon became apparent that if a teacher bottled up the stress, it would explode vociferously sometime in the summer term, either through illness or breakdown.

'I now teach at a mixed Church of England technology college in a small village in Lancashire. It is only ten minutes from my previous school and contains many pupils with the same background. Classroom management is not a problem here as pupils are motivated, interested and enjoy learning. Parental pressure and expectations are high on both pupils and teachers. Although it may seem that my stress levels have decreased, in fact my stress comes in a very different form here. Pupils and teachers must achieve. My lessons were observed and critically examined four times in my first term. Perfect record-keeping is essential, and takes up a great deal of time. As classes are taught in mixed ability groups, lesson planning takes a long time and is carefully monitored. Teachers who face any problems are told to deal with them (alone) in a fast and efficient manner. I seem to have less spare time now, especially as I live 45 miles from the college.

'In order to relax, I have devised a strategy. While driving to school, early so as to miss all the traffic, I go through what I have to do that day. I get to school an hour before classes start and therefore have ample time to fill myself with caffeine and organize resources for the day ahead. Driving home, after numerous meetings and telephone calls to pupils' homes, I evaluate the day and prioritize the evening ahead. After driving for 40 minutes, my mind is no longer on school but on what to have for dinner. I still have not been able to get rid of the need to talk my day through with someone else and therefore I blabber on useless, uninteresting information to my partner when I get home. It does not matter if he is listening as long as he nods, smiles and makes sympathetic noises in the right places. I have also got two dogs. Evening walks are essential for both me and them. Fresh air circulating the brain, thinking about nothing other than why one of the dogs won't stop sniffing that tree.

'Taking time off at weekends is difficult because there is always something to do, but I cannot let school be the priority of my life and have begun to make time doing other things – shopping, socializing, watching television, decorating the house.

'Stress levels vary at different times of the year and change according to the circumstances in which you work. Wherever you work, teaching is not simply lots of holidays.'

Further education

'After working in industry for many years, finally as a trainer, I decided to pursue a career in teaching at a college of further education.

'The first year was fairly basic and I enjoyed preparing lectures, helping students, arranging visits to a variety of industrial establishments, inviting guest speakers into the college and organizing and monitoring work experience. Practical sessions and role play were particularly useful and many of these were videoed for analysing.

'Over the next two years I gained a teaching qualification, studying part-time in addition to teaching. This brought on a little stress as some of my teaching notes and handouts were not updated and I didn't feel as professional as I thought I should.

'Gaining promotion at college brought many additional responsibilities including timetabling, rooming, interviewing and representing the department on two college committees. On several occasions I had to leave students with work to research on their own. I had no control over when certain meetings took place, and of course this appeared to be more important than the teaching, but I wasn't happy with that. Students were encouraged to find their own work placements, many of which were unsuitable, but were at least convenient. Visits had long gone and guest speakers were a thing of the past.

'For several years I looked after all the student induction throughout the department. Many of the lecturers didn't want to get involved, they were always too busy. It was hard work sorting out different activities for the new students. Someone else wanted to do the induction one year. It didn't work very well but they were "flavour of the month" so great thanks went to this particular person. I felt the lack of recognition for my efforts really upsetting. Soon afterwards, I found an expenses claim form for my head of department. I knew that he hadn't spent that amount of money because he hadn't been involved in the two projects that he was claiming for. I had. I lost respect for this person, and the college lost £100. I couldn't say anything to anyone and this didn't help matters.

'It was about this time that the college became increasingly aware of costs, hours, student retention and size of groups. It was also brought to my attention that the students applying for places on the courses on offer did not have the relevant qualifications. By this stage everyone was beginning to worry about their subject areas and began to relax the entry requirements. My colleagues and I had already seen the closure of two departments and, following the merger of another, everyone was feeling that the only way forward was to accept any students that appeared to be interested in our line of work and to help them as much as possible. We now had students on courses they were not qualified for, they were unable to cope with the workload and many were either dropping out or missing lessons. When I first began interviewing students for the courses, we had 70–80 applicants for a course with only 20 places, so we made sure that the selection procedure was followed accurately and usually we had 100 per cent achievement. Now that the courses are not so specialized, many programme areas fight for the same students.

'Many lecturers asked for support from management and this was not forthcoming. Management wasn't very good at telling us new policies. I felt isolated. The college management didn't care for my well-being at all. Lecturers thought at this time that they were being blamed for any student failures. Next came the discussions, "Should we pass Sally? She hasn't attended as she should, not all of her work is of the standard we usually require, but she is a nice girl and she does try." Or, "Do we fail her as we should and look at our achievements at the end of the year?" It was fairly clear what the outcome would be.

'Next came inspection, redundancies both voluntary and compulsory followed closely, more cuts, bigger group sizes. It was at this time I realized my home life was beginning to suffer and I began to suffer with a minor illness. It was something very irritating but would not get better despite different medication from my local GP. I was referred to a specialist who after three consultations diagnosed stress. I felt guilty staying at home and putting my work colleagues under pressure. I also felt guilty when I went into college as the students didn't trust me anymore.

'Eighteen months down the line I teach part-time at another college. I discuss my availability each term and negotiate my hours. I help out at my daughter's school assisting a boy with learning difficulties.

'Last month I took a group of students on a visit and we are planning another in the near future. I look at the full-time lecturers and the problems are still there, the stress and the workload. They do not appear to have any quality of life. I do not get involved with the politics of the department, I teach my class, mark their work, submit the grades and go home. More importantly, my classnotes and questions are up to date and I feel a lot better being in control.'

Higher education

'Coming into teaching in higher education after 20 years in local government, including jobs in town planning, I might have thought that work would be less stressful. Little did I know! In fact, coming from an academic family, I suppose I was well aware of the peculiar and rather insular culture of university and had read enough "campus" novels (Lodge, Bradbury) to be forewarned.

'In many ways, compared with jobs that explicitly and obviously are seen as stressful (emergency services, health, police, social care), teaching in higher education can be and is only stressful when workloads are really heavy and unfairly shared out. My teaching workload has been heavily geared towards post-graduate teaching in management related subjects, many being MBA subjects. For others this could be stressful, but for me it is enjoyable and challenging.

'This underlines the importance of being clear about one's goals and objectives, and especially of not losing sight of the key learning outcomes of a session, a module, an assessment. It helps particularly not to let students put the teacher on a pedestal, or to expect an expertise that is simply not possible or appropriate. As a former manager, former student (including an MBA) and current consultant (in addition to my lecturing), I have tried to see my teaching from the student's view point. I can remember coming to evening classes after a long and hard day's work. I can remember the fear of negative assessments from staff who I felt had less experience in the field than I and my fellow students had! It used to be galling to hear teachers pronounce on some topic of management even though there was evidently no personal experience to support the statements made. Worst of all, teachers seemed afraid to mobilize the resources of students themselves as learning partners, by making their teaching more participative and interactive.

'So being a poacher turned gamekeeper helps! But it can, perversely, be stressful when students fail to take advantage of such open-ended and participative learning, looking for more "content" or some panacea for a set of management problems.

'The important thing is to take opportunities to be creative, to take risks in teaching, such as getting students out of their comfort zone about their learning, but be streetwise about the various responses you may get. It's a bit like defensive thinking – "what if" is a useful coping strategy.

'For me, the best coping strategy is to be up front at the beginning of the programme, the model, the class, about learning objectives and outcomes. Then both lecturer and students can refer to these as justification of what is being looked for, even if a member of the "awkward squad" does not!

'Stress is therefore a personal thing. One person's stress is another person's challenge. Having been exhaustively checked, prodded and probed for my learning style, personality type and team roles (plus what my partner tells me), I know I find doing anything for the first time difficult and stressful but I'll do it – and then it becomes enjoyable until it becomes too routine.

'My tips for reducing stress in teaching can be divided roughly into "preparation" and "delivery" factors. By preparation, I mean the planning, designing, accrediting and testing of teaching material in the programme. This can be stressful and might include confirming you have a room to teach in! The six 'P's come to mind as a useful guide, but to be polite I reduce these to five: "proper planning prevents poor performance".

'The delivery factors centre on the inherent variety built into the actual teaching experience: does the overhead projector bulb go the first minute, someone is having a bad day (and is sharing it with us), the joke that went down well yesterday went down like a lead balloon today. . .! I suppose my approach to stress in this environment is to be human and share it. Being a control freak and/or an expert is not likely to help! Being a facilitator and just trying to do one's best is something that gets students on your side.

'Underpinning all of these factors are, I think, basic ways of reducing stress. By having a balanced lifestyle. In my case, this means plenty of physical exercise to allow me to unwind or prepare as needed. Running, swimming and cycling are, depending on the time of year, activities I find time for in my diary in order to reduce stress. I find that, even on the busiest day, it is possible to do something.'

Teaching in the USA

Allen is a high school teacher from a city within Los Angeles, California.

'I mainly teach math, although I have taught psychology, sociology and English. Although I teach high school, I also teach in downtown Los Angeles on Saturdays and some evenings. Students are completely different. At high school, the students range in age from 16–18 and most are from middle- to upper-class backgrounds, coming to school in their own cars and always fashionably dressed. My downtown students are mostly part-time, many are immigrants and usually over the age of 20.

'Many of my problems come from the high school environment, which in LA doesn't give much recognition to vocational subjects. Some students are not suited to a higher level of academic work but they cannot graduate without math and English. It would be much better for the students and the teachers if vocational areas were promoted and job skills were taught alongside some realistic level of academic subjects. Trying to get students who have difficulty with a simple calculation through a final math exam causes a great deal of stress for all of us.

'Although I now have a doctorate qualification, this is not recognized because it was attained through what the assessment board refers to as an inadequate school that isn't accredited. This is another reason for my stress. It gets very tough when the qualifications you work for are not acknowledged and you know that the assessment board panel is made up of people without the same level of subject knowledge. What right have they to doubt my qualifications?

'I have a number of ways for dealing with stress. Some are in class and some are more about my home life. I make sure that I have "personal time" when I do things for myself and my family. I think that it is important to make space for myself and for my work. I like to keep physically active and play sports and exercise as much as possible.

'In school I think of myself not as a disciplinarian but I do need to keep control. Trust and faith are important, as well as the need to recognize mature students. Most of the students have both parents working and so they need to be self-disciplined. In the past I have tried to involve the parents by inviting them to the school in the evening, but most don't show up. The employment contracts are re-negotiated yearly and are usually about one year behind. Although pay increases are back dated, it usually is a year to 18 months late. This often causes a lot of stress and some teachers are very sensitive about how much they earn. It creates a feeling of uncertainty, which doesn't help.

'Average class size is 41 although I have taught 49 before now. It gets frustrating. It's not so much the teaching that's the problem, but the grading and assessment for the students' papers. There isn't usually a limit on class size and the students just sign up for a class. Most rooms have 35 seats and the same number of books. The school usually asks for volunteers to postpone a particular class until the next semester but they don't guarantee that the same class will run. This puts teachers in a difficult position. I don't like a large class but I don't like to turn someone away from a class that they want to do, especially without a guarantee that they will get another chance. School counsellors (careers advisors) aren't really sympathetic. One more student to them doesn't really matter, and doesn't seem overwhelming. But one, and then another one and so on, soon becomes a problem. Sometimes we combine classes if they get really big, such as English and social studies. However, we get twice as long classes so that doesn't really solve the problem. The lowest level of math I teach is algebra 1. Some students haven't got foundation and have a problem with calculators, decimals and fractions. They reach for a calculator in the same way that they reach for a dictionary, but with no concept of math it makes it difficult. They believe the calculator whatever the result.

'The reasons for the stress are made clear to the board of education but they are not always addressed. Many are district employees with knowledge about business but no knowledge about education. They sit in their ivory tower. Some teachers are the same. Those now in a position of authority sometimes forget or lose sight of what we are doing. They are not very kindly.

'I think the school board is missing the boat by not doing apprenticeship programmes together with a level of math and English. There are fewer vocational classes than before, such as woodwork, metalwork, automobile etc. yet there should be for those who are not bright. The main focus is to gain academic competence. Over 70 per cent have low grades in Math, "D" – "F", but they need a "C" to graduate.'

Teaching in a Japanese school

Yukari teaches in a high school in Japan.

'The culture is very different in my country. It is very strict. Most times there are about 40 students in the class. The classes are graded according to ability. Sometimes they are called King Class or Queen Class. In every class the students have homework and tests. There are tests four times each year. The tests are from memory. If the students pass, they go up to the higher class. If they fail, they can repeat the test two more times. If they fail, they stay in the same class. If a student fails the test three times, they are expelled. Most of the students want to achieve for their friends and their family. It is a great dishonour to be expelled. The students have to give the teacher the work by the deadline. If they do not, they are punished. Teachers are well respected and the students only speak when they are spoken to. The students listen and take note.

'We don't suffer from stress in the same way that I have found since coming to Europe. Here the students answer back and show little respect for the teacher. Where I am now working the students don't seem to care about failing. They don't see passing or failing as we do in Japan. We are much more competitive at school but here students get another chance, and another and another, so there is not the same pressure on them to do well at first.

'At home in Japan, I do sometimes have difficulties with my students but not as many problems. When I do, I can discuss it with the headteacher or the parents of the student. I enjoy my work in Japan and, because teachers are respected, I get support from my friends and family and we spend a lot of time together.'

Another case study from the USA

The setting

'I teach in a school of social work within the setting of a research university that places great emphasis on research productivity, scholarly work, teaching at the graduate, professional level and service to the university and to the community. Like any research university in the United States today, state legislators are demanding more accountability in the area of teaching while the university culture still prizes research work and research productivity. Of course, students evaluate your work on the basis of its relevance and responsiveness to them, and community organizations want more service from professors as well as more relevance from them.

'I highlight this setting only to underscore that the modern (or should I say the "post-modern") professor must respond to a diversity of constituencies in a highly charged environment in which somewhat countervailing expectations surround and influence the role of a public university faculty member. My institution must deal with considerable diversity in expectations, a setting that can produce high levels of stress even among the heartiest members of the professorial ranks.'

Type of students

'This diversity is most apparent among the students. I teach, serve, and undertake research in a large urban university. Students come to the university for undergraduate, pre-professional, and graduate and professional education, and they come with many different aspirations, expectations, and issues. Some students are very autonomous and prepared to undertake their education while others are not well prepared in an academic sense. Nonetheless they have a considerable number of strengths that lie in motivation, commitment, curiosity, and life experience. Numerous students are the first in their families to pursue higher education, while other students are coming back to the academy after a long period of absence. Still other students are coming to advance their economic status.

'The diversity of the students is seen in their life styles, demographics, and cultures. But they share three things in common. First, they have high hopes for what they can achieve through education. Second, they want to be the centre of their education. And, third, they want faculty members to focus their energy on them. They do not really care about the faculty member's research commitments or their publishing priorities. For these students, the measure of quality of a public university is its responsiveness to them. Since the faculty member is the primary representative of the institution, students look to the professor as the person who is accountable for their education.'

Reasons for my stress in education

'Forgive me. I do not want to sound like I am whining. I know about this kind of teaching quite well. I earned my doctorate in one of the world's largest research universities. As a doctoral student, I was responsible for teaching at the undergraduate level while my mentors pursued more "important forms" of professorial life like preparing proposals, pursuing research, and publishing and disseminating their findings. But perhaps one of the reasons for my stress is that I did not see any mentors who successfully integrated all the expectations that higher education places on faculty members today. The institution where I received my doctoral education was very clear that research came first. Yet, even this institution must now prioritize teaching and service in this new environment of countervailing expectations.

'My present institution wants good, if not great, teaching. It wants relevant and sustainable research, particularly research that brings in funds. It wants service to the university, to the community, and to the profession that the faculty member represents. Students want other things, but most of all they want a faculty member who is focused, centred, and who has the energy to respond to their needs on an individualized basis.

'The expectations can go on and on. Often they clash at evaluation time, whether for salary advancement, tenure, or promotion. The main question is whether the faculty member performs in all venues and whether every constituency is well satisfied with how the faculty member performs. Stress is built into the role of the professor. Most professors cannot escape it.

'Of course, many readers will say that this is merely classical role strain and the degree of stress a faculty member experiences is directly related to the extent to which he or she tries to perform well in each domain. Well, role strain comes with the job, particularly when we factor in self-expectations. Many of my colleagues, myself included, feel that professorial work is a form of public service. We want to make sure that the public receives value for its investment in higher education. So I know that I am not alone in feeling stress created by trying to make sure that professorial work is relevant, productive, and effective.'

Examples of stressful situations

'Three situations in my career illuminate how countervailing expectations conspire to create stress.

'When I was an untenured faculty member, I remember well trying to juggle teaching responsibilities with my efforts to undertake research and scholarly work. I can remember juggling my day so that I could take care of teaching and administrative duties within so-called normal working hours while trying to reserve time in the evening for writing and research. I really did become adept at juggling but I am not sure that I was very focused on all of my duties. As my research agenda expanded, my teaching quality decreased (at least this is how I felt). I think that the stress here came in the form of trying to meet my own expectations, and my appraisal of just how good (or not good) I was performing in each of the key areas the university defined as important was influential to how much stress I felt. When things piled up, when support was low, my appraisal was negative and I can remember having some stomach aches. When support was high, my energy fresh, well then, my appraisal was positive. Appraisal is an important factor in the management of stress.

'Early in my career, I could get away with classroom-based teaching in a lecture format. From my perspective, student expectations about the diversity, form, and experiential-base of teaching changed somewhere in the mid-1990s. My graduate students wanted to pursue their own interests and shape assignments more around their aims than my own. Although I welcomed this form of assertiveness, fulfilling these expectations did not lend itself to efficient forms of mass education. I found myself needing to spend more and more time on crafting relevant assignments, linking classroom-based education to clinical forms of education, and facilitating student involvement in more individualized directed studies.

'The emergence of electronic forms of education offers me more tools for educating professionals and they make the process more efficient. But, responding to students in a rich, relevant, and individualized format creates stress, particularly when you have a number of students. In addition, as I invest more in teaching, I find the pull of research to mount. Stress comes from trying to meet many different "masters" but if I did not perceive teaching and research to have equal value then I probably could reduce the stress I do experience tremendously. Choices and commitments matter in the experience of stress.

'The competition for students in higher education is becoming increasingly intensive here in the States. Distance education options, part-time programmes, Internet degrees, and alternative adult education programmes in higher education give students many different options. The emphasis on student retention and persistence in most universities means that faculty members cannot just stand up and "profess". They have to monitor students, link them to services, and facilitate their development. They have to identify at-risk students, and help students to re-enter programmes after they resolve major life crises. I am closer to most of my students than ever in my teaching career in higher education. I know a lot about their family lives, their personal and financial situations, and the issues they have to deal with. It is not unusual for five or six of my students to be on the brink of crisis during the course of a semester. Fortunately, I am educated as a social worker so these issues do not overwhelm me. But I do experience stress in trying to make university life work for these students and to teach them how to work the university to achieve situations that are productive for them. So, not only am I a researcher, educator, curriculum leader, and scholar, but I also serve as a student advocate. Stress does originate from my efforts to personalize the education of my students. I am the face of public higher education and I have to keep this in the forefront of my mind.'

Personal coping strategies

'Although numerous environmental and institutional forces can induce stress, it is really up to faculty members to learn how to manage and care for themselves. One of my key strategies is to always, and I mean always, keep in mind how important professorial work is, and to keep at the forefront of my mind what I define as my sense of professorial duty. This cognitive orientation offers me a sense of empowerment, that is, it helps me to feel in control of my world and the decisions I make about my work. Of course, I need a support system and so I find my small group of scholarly friends and colleagues critical to the achievement of balance and perspective.

'An example is my friend Shirley, who passed away almost five years ago. Before her illness, we met once a week for dinner just to discuss and explore our perspectives on teaching, research, and service. Our dinner meetings were always punctuated by humour as we reflected on what went well with our work, and what did not go well. Our humour allowed us to express the stress we were feeling and we would always end mindful of the forces that brought us into teaching. Through this friendship with someone who "knew the business of higher education", I could reaffirm my commitment to a life of teaching and learning. I view this commitment as an asset that I have groomed and developed over a period of almost 25 years of teaching in higher education.

'There are other coping strategies that I employ. Reading literature authored by people who teach always gives me ideas about how to develop my pedagogical or andragogical skills. I am always delighted to find book-length treatments of teaching and of autobiographical works on teaching. These authors remind me that I am not alone and that ultimately teaching means giving (and giving) and the sharing of yourself with others who want to take away something just for themselves (which students often do). The interpersonal context of teaching demands much of professors and is stressful. But it is also beneficial to the spirit. Ultimately, good teaching and good research are forms of service. When I read books on teaching I reflect on the great teachers I was honoured to have (as if they belonged to me alone). Seeing great teaching in action helps aspiring professors to form positive images of professorial practice, and these images are potential buffers against stress. Call one up and reflect on it. Explore it. Mediate about it. These images offer healing and they can help a weary educator to get back on their path. Readers can see that I depend on cognitive imagery to cope with stress. This imagery supplemented by relaxation and mediation are coping resources that can strengthen us when we feel most vulnerable.

'I cherish my role as a professor and its great scope and responsibility. Reading the works of John Dewey reminds me of the spiritual duty I must fulfil as an educator. So ultimately I manage my stress by accepting who I am and what I must do. I get tired at times. And, I get depressed or even angry when I think that people want too much of me. But usually depression and anger occur at a time when I am most weary. When this occurs, I rely on the ultimate remedies: rest, sleep, chocolate, and losing myself in the cinema! After all, even professors have other lives.'

Appendix 2: Measure your own stress at school, college or university

Table A. 1 How to measure your stress

	Rarely or never stressed		Stressful		A great deal of stress	
Student behaviour	0	1	2	3	4	5
Job knowledge	0	1	2	3	4	5
Conditions of service	0	1	2	3	4	5
Management decision-making	0	1	2	3	4	5
Too many meetings	0	1	2	3	4	5
Role ambiguity	0	1	2	3	4	5
Job interfering with family life	0	1	2	3	4	5
Resources	0	1	2	3	4	5
Lack of work	0	1	2	3	4	5
Lack of opportunity	0	1	2	3	4	5
Change	0	1	2	3	4	5
Communication	0	1	2	3	4	5
Unclear guidelines	0	1	2	3	4	5
Lack of parental support	0	1	2	3	4	5

Total all your scores. The following is a rough guide to your stress level at work:

50–70 You are suffering from a great deal of stress and should seek help.
30–50 Some aspects of your work are stressful. Identify high scoring areas and draw upon a coping strategy as detailed in Chapters 5 and 6.
10–30 You are under some pressure at work but this is not proving difficult.
Under 10 Few pressures. Are you in teaching?

Appendix 3: Research

Much of the research for this book has been carried out in consultation with teachers in schools, colleges and universities. As part of this, they were asked two questions; responses are summarized below.

Question 1. In your experience, what causes stress in education?

bad management;
staff employment conditions;
lack of subject knowledge;
excessive workload;
lack of time;
excessive paperwork;
inadequate resources;
too many meetings and not enough action;
lack of parental support;
poor communication systems;
lack of discipline;
lack of common courtesies/respect/manners;
lack of support;
unqualified management;
lack of recognition.

Question 2. What do you feel could be done to reduce stress in education?

standardization;
praise, not criticism;
more resources;
more information filtering;
time management for ourselves;

get things into perspective... this is a job, not my life;
management should *listen* to its staff;
communication should be clearer from all managers;
effective and participative management;
trust;
more staff recognition;
insist that senior managers have management training;
lesson preparation;
continual change;
decisions made too late... crisis management;
endless meetings at which nothing is decided.

Index

Visit Kogan Page on-line

Comprehensive information on
Kogan Page titles

Features include

- complete catalogue listings,
  including book reviews and
  descriptions

- on-line discounts on a variety
  of titles

- special monthly promotions

- information and discounts on
  NEW titles and BESTSELLING titles

- a secure shopping basket facility
  for on-line ordering

- infoZones, with links and
  information on specific areas of
  interest

PLUS everything you need to know
about KOGAN PAGE

http://www.kogan-page.co.uk